Nethermost

MISSIONARY MIRACLES IN LOWLY PLACES

Francis M. Gibbons
Daniel Bay Gibbons

Sixteen Stones Press

HOLLADAY, UTAH

Sixteen Stones Press
6289 Howey Drive
Holladay, Utah 84121
www.sixteenstonespress.com

Sixteen Stones Press logo design by Marina Teležar
Cover design by Daliborka Mijailovic
Book Layout and Typography ©2013 BookDesignTemplates.com

Ordering Information:
Quantity sales. Special discounts are available on quantity purchases by corporations, associations, and others. For details, contact Sixteen Stones Press at the address above.

Nethermost: Missionary Miracles in Lowly Places/ by Francis M. Gibbons and Daniel Bay Gibbons. —1st ed.
ISBN 978-0-9906387-0-4

Contents

PART ONE
"IT MAY NOT BE ON THE MOUNTAIN HEIGHT"

PART TWO
"OVER THE STORMY SEA"

PART THREE
"AT THE BATTLE'S FRONT"

PART FOUR
"IF, BY A STILL SMALL VOICE HE CALLS"

PART FIVE
"PERHAPS TODAY THERE ARE LOVING WORDS"

PART SIX
"SOME WANDE'RER WHOM I SHOULD SEEK"

To the two hundred and forty-nine
Elders, Sisters, and Senior Missionaries
of the Russia Novosibirsk Mission
who served in Siberia and Kazakhstan
July 1, 2011 to July 1, 2014

It may not be on the mountain height
Or over the stormy sea,
It may not be at the battle's front
My Lord will have need of me.
But if, by a still, small voice he calls
To paths that I do not know,
I'll answer, dear Lord, with my hand in thine:
I'll go where you want me to go.

Perhaps today there are loving words
Which Jesus would have me speak;
There may be now in the paths of sin
Some wand'rer whom I should seek.
O Savior, if thou wilt be my guide,
Tho dark and rugged the way,
My voice shall echo the message sweet:
I'll say what you want me to say.

There's surely somewhere a lowly place
In earth's harvest fields so wide
Where I may labor through life's short day
For Jesus, the Crucified.
So trusting my all to thy tender care,
And knowing thou lovest me,
I'll do thy will with a heart sincere:
I'll be what you want me to be.

—Hymn 270

Part One

"IT MAY NOT BE
ON THE MOUNTAIN HEIGHT"

*It may not be on the mountain height
Or over the stormy sea,
It may not be at the battle's front
My Lord will have need of me.
But if, by a still, small voice he calls
To paths that I do not know,
I'll answer, dear Lord, with my hand in thine:
I'll go where you want me to go.*

—Hymn 270, Verse 1

CHAPTER ONE

Nethermost and Condescension
by Daniel Bay Gibbons

There are two words in scripture which are bound so inextricably together that they might as well be two sides of the same coin.

The words are *Nethermost* and *Condescension*. These words both appear in *The Book of Mormon* and are rich with meaning.

The word *Nethermost* is found only in Jacob, chapter 5, which is a great allegory of the gathering of Israel in the last days. We read of a great vineyard filled with olive trees, some tame and many wild. The Master of the vineyard, however, has one favorite tree, planted in the best spot. In time, His favorite tree begins to grow old and to decay. In order to save the tree, the Master of the vineyard instructs his servants to prune its branches and graft in their place other branches taken from wild olive trees. The Master of the vineyard is about to burn the natural branches of his favorite tree, but then changes his mind. He tells His servants to take the "young and tender branches," which they have just pruned, and carry them to "the nethermost part of the vineyard" and there graft them into other wild olive trees. After many years, the Master of the vineyard sees that his favorite tree has become corrupt and has ceased to bring forth good fruit. He considers whether to cut down his beloved tree, but then decides to try one more experiment. He instructs his servants to return to "the nethermost parts of the vineyard" to see what has become of the natural branches of his beloved tree. And the servants go and see that the natural branches are thriving and bringing forth good fruit. So the Master of the vineyard and his servants return to "the nethermost part of the vineyard." There they gather the natural branches, bring them back, and graft them back into their mother tree. There they once again bring forth good fruit.

In the *Oxford English Dictionary*, we learn that *Nethermost* is a very ancient word, coming to us from the Old English, with literary roots dating back to the ninth century. *Nethermost* means "lowest," "undermost," or "furthest down." It is often applied to localities, such as countries, districts, hamlets, and farms. *Nethermost* also is used anciently to distinguish heaven from the earth or from the "netherworld" or "underworld" or world of the departed dead. This is what we would call in Mormon thought "the spirit world."

Nethermost thus means the lowest and most removed place. In each of our lives there are low points, valleys, sorrows, trials, setbacks, betrayals, disappointments, stumbling blocks, and closed doors. We all face illness, adversity, rock-bottom experiences, and ultimately death. Psalm 23:4 speaks of walking "through the valley of the shadow of death." We all one day must walk through that *Nethermost* valley.

The word *Condescension* is also a *Book of Mormon* word, appearing in many places, including in 1 Nephi 11. There we read that an angel asks Nephi, "Knowest thou the condescension of God?" to which Nephi responds, "I know that he lovest his children, nevertheless I do not know the meaning of all things." Nephi then sees the birth of the Savior to Mary. The angel then proclaims, "Behold the condescension of God!" and Nephi looks and witnesses the baptism of the Savior, at the hands of John the Baptist, and then His earthly ministry.

In the *Oxford English Dictionary* we learn that *Condescension* comes from the ancient Latin root word *scandere*, which means "to climb, to walk or to leap." Added to this root are the Latin prefixes *con-*, meaning "with," and *de-*, meaning "down." Thus, *Condescend* literally means, "to walk down with." Other modern English words that are derived from scandere are *ascend* (meaning "to walk or climb up"), *descend* (meaning "to walk or climb down") and *transcend* (meaning "to walk or leap across"). *Condescend* means "to walk down with," "to come down from one's rights or privileges," "to come down voluntarily," "to come down or bend down from one's position of dignity," or "to stoop voluntarily and graciously." These, of course, are perfect descriptions of the ministry of Jesus Christ. He voluntarily came down upon the earth to "walk with" us in order to save us and lift us up.

The earliest fragment of Christian writing in the New Testament is found in Paul's epistle to the Philippians. This epistle is itself one of the earliest New Testament texts, having been written decades before any of the Gospels. In Philippians 2:6-11, Paul quotes what was already by that time an old Christian hymn, called the *Kenosis Hymn*. This hymn is a kind of "literary fossil" embedded in the ancient text of Philippians. It refers to the *Nethermost* places and also to the *Condescension* of Jesus Christ, and reads:

He was divine,
yet He did not cling
to his equality with God,
but He emptied himself
to assume the condition of a slave
and became as men are;
and being as men are,
he was humbler yet,
even to accepting death,
upon the cross.
But God lifted him up
and gave him a Name
which is above all other names,
so that among all creations
in the heavens, and on the earth
and in the nethermost place,
every knee shall bow at the name of Jesus
and every tongue confess
that Jesus is the Christ,
to the glory of God the Father.
(My translation of Philippians 2:6-12)

The grand principles of *Nethermost* and *Condescension* are inextricably linked, like two sides to the same coin. One side describes our lowly and trial-filled condition in life; the other side depicts the Savior of mankind, who voluntarily "walks down with us" through those trials and brings us safely through. One of my favorite *Book of Mormon* scriptures also describes both sides of the coin:

> O then, if I have seen so great things, if the Lord in his condescension unto the children of men hath visited men in so much mercy, why should my heart weep and my soul linger in the valley of sorrow? (2 Nephi 4:26)

Remember how the angel said to Nephi, "Behold the condescension of God," and then immediately showed him the baptism of Christ? Baptism is one of the most powerful symbols of our *Nethermost* state in life and the *Condescension* of Jesus Christ. In the ordinance of baptism we see a short visual and dramatic depiction of the condescension of Christ. All ordinances combine covenant making with visual or dramatic depictions of gospel principles. This is true with the sacrament, with the anointing of consecrated oil, with the ordinances of the temple, and with baptism. In the ordinance of baptism, we see a man dressed in white walk down into a place below ground, filled with water, with the baptismal candidate, who is also dressed in white. The man in white then addresses the person by name, states that he is "commissioned of Jesus Christ," and that he is baptizing the person "in the name of the Father, and of the Son, and of the Holy Ghost." The candidate is then submersed in the water, which is a cleansing agent, but also a place of potential peril, for we cannot breathe underwater. Then, at the lowest place and moment, the man in white lifts the candidate out of the water to take a new breath and to begin a new life.

The sacred ordinance of baptism is emblematic of how the atonement of Christ operates in our lives. At our lowest and darkest moments, when we are in moments of peril, unable to breathe, at our wit's end, at rock bottom, we find that Christ is already at our side, ready to reach out his hand and lift us up.

I have seen the operation of the *Condescension* of God in the *Nethermost* part of the vineyard of the Lord. *Nethermost* is a phrase especially appropriate for the Russia Novosibirsk Mission, where I served for three wonderful years with my eternal companion, Julie Glenn Gibbons. It is the most removed mission on earth. It is a land of both great beauty and great sadness. It is a place where the blood of Israel is very strong. It is a place where the natural branches of the olive tree are thriving, and ready to be grafted into their mother tree.

This book is a kind of meditation upon the concept of *Nethermost* things and *Nethermost* places, and how the *Condescension* of God operates in those places to bring about the atonement of Jesus Christ. My father and I will share our personal experiences in passing through the *Nethermost* places in our personal lives and in going forth in the ministry to the *Nethermost* parts of the vineyard in North America, South America, Europe, Russia, and Central Asia, as well as drawing from the treasure trove of Church history.

This book is dedicated to the two hundred and forty-nine missionaries who served with my wife, Julie, and me in Russia and Central Asia. It is our hope that this little book may be a help to them and to other missionaries and members who go into *Nethermost* places to proclaim the *Condescension* of Jesus Christ.

CHAPTER TWO

"Your Father Appeared to Me"
by Francis M. Gibbons

My father, Judge Andrew Smith Gibbons, died in December 1940 at age sixty as the result of injuries he suffered when a car struck him as he walked across the street in downtown Phoenix, Arizona. When my sister Pauline called at my office at the headquarters of the A. J. Bayless Markets to tell me of the accident, the thought came to me instantly that my father would never recover, a thought which persisted during the following days, even though he was released from the hospital and was reported to be recovering.

At the time of his death, I was nineteen years old and had worked at the Bayless office for almost two years as a bookkeeper and clerk. I had previously worked for several years for the same grocery chain, while a student, as a combination cashier and stock clerk in its stores. During my student years, I worked three hours a night, Monday through Friday and from 6:00 a.m. Saturday until midnight. Also, every first Sunday, we took an inventory of the store, which made it necessary for me to work from 8:00 a.m. to mid-afternoon. This schedule made it impossible for me to attend priesthood meeting at least once each month and difficult the other Sundays because of my eighteen-hour schedule on Saturdays. Under these circumstances, my parents had refrained from pressing me to attend priesthood meeting on Sundays when I did not work and, left to my own initiative, I became dilatory in attending, even when there was no valid excuse for not doing so. These slovenly habits had carried over even when I began to work in the Bayless office, when it was never necessary for me to work on Sunday. Therefore, I was very erratic in attending priesthood meeting, going only when it suited my convenience.

It was against this background that Mother came to my bedroom early one Sunday morning shortly after my father was buried. She was in a high state of excitement and said to me with the greatest urgency: "Frank, your father just appeared to me and said, 'Go get the boy up and get him to priesthood meeting!'"

Whether it was a dream my mother had, or whether it was an actual appearance of my father in spiritual form, I do not know. What I do know is that it had a profound influence on my mother, as it did on me, for I promptly heeded the instruction, arose, dressed, and went to priesthood meeting. During the many years that have intervened since that day, I have consistently attended priesthood meetings, except in instances when illness, travel or other church assignments have precluded me from doing so.

CHAPTER THREE

"I Thought My Mission was a Failure"

by Daniel Bay Gibbons

I had two mission presidents in the Germany Duesseldorf Mission from 1976 to 1978: first, President Hans-Juergen Saager, the first West German citizen ever called as a mission president, and second, Robert H.M. Killpack, a former stake president then residing in Murray, Utah. I had the privilege of serving as an assistant to the president under each of these great men, and learned much from them. Near the conclusion of my mission, President Saager concluded his three years of service and was released and President Killpack arrived in Germany with his family.

I remember the mild culture shock that swept the mission with the arrival of the new president. Under the German mission president there was a culture of exact obedience and rule following to an extraordinary degree. For example, we never called each other nicknames, like "guys," and in fact, never used the familiar form of address with each other in the German language. Also, all elders in the mission wore identical dark-blue German-tailored suits with "Seidensticker" brand white shirts, whose chief quality was an almost indestructible stiff white collar. American tailored suits, especially brown ones, were frowned upon, as were American white shirts, which were derisively called "noodles" because of their limp collars, in comparison to the rigid Seidenstickers.

So, imagine our astonishment when my companion and I drove to the airport to meet President Killpack and his family, and he greeted us with a cheery, "Hi guys!" wearing a brown American suit and a "noodle!" I turned to my companion and whispered, "This is a new day, Elder."

My companion and I quickly became very close to President Killpack, and he told us much about his first mission to Germany in the months immediately following World War II. He and his companions were the first missionaries to return following the devastation and disruption of the war and spent most of their missions trying to locate lost members and reestablish the old branches of the Church. I remember one story in particular that President Killpack told us. He said that he and his companion traveled by assignment of their mission president to a German city with the task of locating the old LDS meetinghouse. They were given keys to the building, but had no idea what to expect when they arrived. In the city, they found the building, which was boarded up and in a state of utter disuse. They succeeded in opening the building and started the huge task of cleaning it up. In a little closet next to the chapel, they found a box containing the sacrament cups and plates, but also a collection of Nazi-style armbands bearing the words "Diakon," "Lehrer," and "Priester," which are the German names for the offices of the Aaronic Priesthood, "Deacon," "Teacher" and "Priest." President Killpack's speculation was that the young brethren wore the armbands during the administration of the sacrament during the dark war-years.

In a long conversation I had with President Killpack one day in the mission office, he confided one sadness of his mission to Germany. Though he served for thirty months in Germany, he and his companions experienced no baptisms. He told me that though he had served as a branch president and had helped locate hundreds of lost members during his mission, he always felt a certain sense of failure about the fact that he had been unable to bring anyone to the waters of baptism.

Against this backdrop occurred the most difficult experience of my mission. A few days after President Killpack's arrival, we received a phone call from one of our district leaders reporting that an Elder named Dieter Fricke, a fairly new German convert from the city of Hannover, had been in a bike accident and was on his way to the hospital in unknown condition. Elder Fricke had only been in the mission field for six weeks. President Killpack had never been to the city where the accident occurred, and so he quickly decided that I would drive him there in his car. The two of us left immediately, and within an hour were at the emergency room of the hospital, where we were surprised to see the entire branch gathered with the handful of elders and sisters. They were all sitting in the waiting room in tears. I went to the district leader and asked him, "How is Elder Fricke?" I'll never forget the unreal feeling I experienced when he looked at me and said, "He's dead!" We then learned that Elder Fricke had been struck by a semi-truck on the highway and killed instantly. His companion, who was following him, was unhurt.

President Killpack quickly gathered the grieving saints and missionaries together for a prayer. He then took me with him to help identify the body and to begin to make arrangements to have the remains sent home.

That evening we drove back to the office in silence, and then called the family of Elder Fricke in Hannover, Germany. They were devastated, as can be imagined, but they were also embittered because they had opposed the baptism of their son and his decision a year later to become a missionary. Because of the tender feelings of the family, President Killpack decided to accompany the body home and to attend the funeral, so as to assuage the feelings of the family as much as possible. President Killpack had served in Hannover during his post-War mission in Germany, and so was curious to see what changes had occurred in the city in the thirty years since his departure.

A few days later, President Killpack returned to the mission and told me this experience. He said that Elder Fricke's funeral was attended by most of the members of the Hannover Stake, and that the family had received some comfort. President Killpack sat on the stand during the funeral and was asked to speak. Following the service, President Killpack was leaving the stand in the midst of a throng of saints when a middle-aged man stopped him and asked, "Do you remember me?"

"No," answered President Killpack. "Have we met?"

"You introduced me to the gospel thirty years ago, and I have wanted all this time to find you and thank you." The man then introduced President Killpack to his wife and to all of his children, who were members of the Church. President Killpack recounted this experience to us with tears in his eyes. He said, "I had never known that my mission had born any fruit at all! I thought my mission was a failure. What a blessing to meet this family, who are the hidden fruit of my mission."

CHAPTER FOUR

"This is Where the Celestial Room Will Be"

by Francis M. Gibbons

In 1972 a tall, regal and intelligent-looking man was baptized a member of the Church in Rio de Janeiro, Brazil. He was a highly successful business executive who, but for the color of his skin, might have been immediately called to some presiding capacity in the growing Church organization in Brazil. Instead, because of the priesthood restrictions then in place, he accepted a calling to clean up the Church grounds. Week after week this new Latter-day Saint, who during the business week directed the work of hundreds of professional workers in the Brazilian National Petroleum Corporation, would cheerfully perform his custodial duties. The joy he and his wife felt when the 1978 revelation on priesthood was announced was overwhelming. Within eighteen years this man, Helvecio Martins, would be called to serve as a member of the Seventy, the first General Authority of African descent in this dispensation.

Born July 27, 1930, in Rio De Janeiro, Brazil, Helvecio Martins grew up as the eldest of nine children in a very poor family. At the age of twelve he was required to go to work to help his parents provide food for the family. He entered the Brazilian military at the age of nineteen and on his return married Ruda Tourinho de Assis.

From the time of his marriage, Helvecio commenced to improve his condition in life and to pursue his education. Gifted with great intellectual capacity, he quickly rose both in the educational and in the business world. He earned the Brazilian equivalent of an American MBA degree, and also completed postgraduate studies in financial administration, personnel management, educational psychology, and public service. He eventually taught economics at the university level and worked in the Brazil National Bank of Economic Development. At the time the missionaries first taught him, he was the director of finance for Petrobras, the Brazilian National Petroleum Corporation.

In all outward respects, life was good to Helvecio and Ruda. They lived in great financial security, enjoyed the highest respect of Helvecio's business associates, and were raising a family of beautiful and gifted children. Both Helvecio and Ruda were Catholic, though they had grown dissatisfied with the teachings of their church and commenced to study other faiths. "We were in a period of confusion," Helvecio recalled. "We felt that something was missing from our lives."

One night in April of 1972, two missionaries from the Church came through the condominium apartment building where the Martins family lived. As is the custom, the missionaries stopped at the security door and used a telephone to call at random some of the families living in the building to ask if they might come in and talk with them. When they called the Martins' home, Ruda Martins felt strongly impressed to invite them in. So impressed were Helvecio and Ruda with the message of the missionaries that they visited from about 8:00 p.m. until almost dawn. Helvecio related that:

> When the missionaries left our home that night, we already had a firm conviction. I already had a testimony of the Church. The missionaries invited us to come to Church on the next Sunday. We went to Church and have not left off going to church from that day

until this. Since that last week of April 1972, until today, we have never missed a Sunday.

Helvecio, Ruda and their oldest son, Marcos, were baptized on July 2, 1972. Helvecio was soon assigned to teach a Sunday School class for investigators of the Church, and Ruda became a counselor in the Primary. Later Helvecio was asked to become the public communications director for the Church in Brazil. In this capacity he appeared on television to explain the mission of the Church. The Martins' son, Marcos, participated fully in the Church with the boys of Aaronic Priesthood age. Notwithstanding the fact that he could not be ordained with them, he never became disaffected or discouraged.

In 1973 Helvecio, Ruda and Marcos received their patriarchal blessings. In Marcos' blessing he was promised that he would one day preach the gospel. "How am I going to be able to preach the gospel if I cannot hold the priesthood?" he asked his father. Helvecio had no answer, but pondered the promise in his heart.

Several years later the First Presidency announced that a temple was to be built in Sao Paulo, Brazil. Helvecio and Ruda contributed generously towards the construction, even though they understood that they would never be allowed to participate in its ordinances. Because of his position as the Church's public communications director in Brazil, Helvecio was frequently called upon to explain the purposes of the temple to the media.

One day while in Sao Paulo, Helvecio and Ruda drove by the construction site of the temple and walked alone through the foundation of the temple. "I think this is where the celestial room will be," Helvecio said to his wife. Tears welled up in his eyes, and the couple clung to each other.

On the day that President Spencer W. Kimball laid the cornerstone of the temple, there was a large gathering of saints in attendance. President Kimball motioned for Helvecio to come up on the stand. At first Helvecio could not imagine why the prophet should beckon to him, and so he looked around to see who the prophet was trying to communicate with. Eventually President Spencer W. Kimball sent Elder James E. Faust down into the audience to lead Helvecio to the stand to sit beside the prophet during the meeting. Helvecio reported that throughout the meeting President Kimball's white hand held on to Helvecio's black hand. At the conclusion of the meeting, President Kimball told Helvecio, "Brother, the word of counsel to you is fidelity. Remain faithful to the Church, and you will enjoy all of its blessings."

On June 23, 1978, soon after the revelation on priesthood was announced by the First Presidency and the Quorum of the Twelve, Helvecio was ordained to the priesthood. Following his ordination, he became a mighty leader in the kingdom, serving first as a mission president in the Brazil Fortaleza Mission, and from 1990 to 1995 as a member of the Second Quorum of the Seventy.

CHAPTER FIVE

The Dog and the Missionary
by Daniel Bay Gibbons

One day in the late 1860's, a large dog chased a man down the streets of Bern, Switzerland. In his haste to elude the dog, the man dropped some papers on the street. Another man, John Kunz, picked up the papers and saw that they were tracts from the Mormon church. From this unlikely beginning, the large Kunz family was ultimately converted to the gospel, immigrated to the United States, and grew into one of the largest families in the Church today.

John Kunz was born on January 2, 1823, in Bern, Switzerland, the son of Johann Kunz and Rosine Catherine Klossner. John was a skilled cheese-maker in Bern. One day as he was walking down the streets of Bern, he saw a large dog chasing a man down the street. The man had a bundle of papers under his arm, and as he ran, some of the papers fell to the cobblestones. Curious, John went over and picked up the papers. They were German language tracts for The Church of Jesus Christ of Latter-day Saints, and the unknown man was a missionary of the Church.

In the coming months John studied the Mormon tracts carefully. Though he never was able to determine the identity of the missionary who dropped the tracts, he ultimately sought out other missionaries of the Church to discuss the things he had read. Within a few years John and most of the members of his numerous extended family were baptized. In the 1870's John immigrated to the United States with his ten children. After arriving at Church headquarters in Salt Lake City, members of the Kunz family made their way to the foothills north of Bear Lake, where they helped settle the little town of Bern, named after their home in Bern, Switzerland. There John Kunz again took up the business of cheese-making. In 1885 John Kunz Jr. returned to Switzerland as a missionary, the first of many hundreds of missionaries to serve from the family. Several generations of Kunzes served as presiding elder or bishop of the little ward in Bern, Idaho, for the next one hundred years. By the end of the twentieth century, the descendants of John Kunz constitute, perhaps, one of the largest families in the Church with many thousands of members.

The Lord frequently moves in mysterious ways, bringing great things to pass from small beginnings. But it is difficult to identify a more humble beginning than a dog chasing a man down a city street. The conversion of the many thousand members of the Kunz family has come from such a beginning.

CHAPTER SIX

Laboring with My Mission President

by Francis M. Gibbons

My father died when I was nineteen years old. I felt his death keenly and yearned for an association with a man of maturity and judgment who could help fill the void created by his passing. It was this yearning, I am sure, which prompted me in the summer of 1942 to begin to pray secretly for the privilege of working with my mission president, William P. Whitaker. These were not prayers for church position, but for an association, in whatever capacity, with a man whom I admired and in whom I saw the potential for a surrogate father relationship. During the course of these inner strugglings, the Spirit whispered to me that my prayers would be answered, a fact which was duly noted in my diary.

President Whitaker travelled to the Florida District in September 1942. Since Elder Hunter was to be released about the same time, High Springs was temporarily closed to missionary work, and I had accompanied Elder Hunter to Jacksonville, from where he travelled home and where I worked temporarily with Elder Jensen and his companion, awaiting reassignment. Unknown to me, President Whitaker had asked Brother Jensen to bring me with him to a meeting to be held in western Florida in Cross City. We drove there early one morning with two brethren from Jacksonville. Following a meeting held in a little chapel, President Whitaker took me aside into a corner of the building and, putting his arm around my shoulders, said he wanted me in the mission office to work as the mission treasurer and supervisor of priesthood. It was a choice moment in my life and I felt then, as I feel now, a great sense of gratitude to my Heavenly Father for answering my prayers and for permitting me to work closely with a spiritual giant like William P. Whitaker.

But this man was also a physical giant. He stood over six feet tall, had a powerful physique, and must have weighed 250 pounds, at least. His ample head of hair was pure white. Everything he did was done with great deliberation. He spoke with a measured cadence whether in a personal conversation or from the pulpit. He walked with a plodding gait, and he ate slowly, savoring each bite with relish. As a young man he had worked on the railroad, and some of his mannerisms and attitudes betrayed that background. But in his later years he became a florist, a business that seemed to be out of kilter with his whole makeup. Yet he loved flowers and flower arrangements, and that quality gave him an appreciation for the beautiful in life.

Another incongruity was that this sensitive florist and decorator loved the hurly burly of politics. For years he had been active in Idaho politics; and not long before his call as the President of the Southern States Mission, he had been a gubernatorial candidate for the Democratic Party. A memorable experience I had while serving as a member of President Whitaker's staff occurred when Utah's democratic United States Senator, Elbert Thomas, came to the mission office seeking a priesthood blessing. The Senator, who was then the Chairman of the Senate Banking Committee, was in Atlanta, Georgia, for a hearing. Having lost his wife recently, he was lonely and despondent and much in need of the spiritual uplift that he felt the priesthood could provide. President Whitaker asked the elders in the office to assist in the blessing. I recall how strange it felt to put my hands on the head of a man who was totally bald. And I recall, too, how impressed I was that this man, who at the time was one of the most powerful men in the

United States government, had the humility and the faith to call on the priesthood for a blessing.

One can imagine what a privilege it was for me, a youth, to be associated on a daily basis with a man of the caliber of William P. Whitaker. He did, indeed, fill the void left by my father's death. And he provided an element, high spirituality, which my father lacked. My father was a mental giant, a genius. Therefore, his approach to life and its problems was usually pitched at the intellectual level. One never heard my father talk about the whisperings of the Spirit, or the promptings of the still small voice, or the power of faith, or the remarkable answers to prayers. A brilliant mathematician, chairman of the mathematics department at Brigham Young University, lawyer, and jurist, he was all mind and intellect. Without question, he was the most brilliant and well-informed man I have ever known. My impression is that he felt it would be a rejection of his unswerving belief in the merits of science and the scientific method were he to speak boldly about something he could not objectively prove or demonstrate. Not so with President Whitaker. Here was a man who governed his life for the most part by things in the spiritual realm. He believed. He had pure faith. His actions usually depended on whether he *felt* it was the right or wrong thing to do in a given situation. Spiritual experiences were almost an everyday occurrence with this man. On one occasion, for instance, at a testimony meeting in Atlanta, he related how, the night before, his mother had appeared to him in open vision. So powerful was the spirit on that occasion that many were in tears, including the President's young son, John.

When I travelled with President Whitaker, which was frequently, we usually shared the same room. We prayed together, studied together, and counseled together about many things, not only about religion, but also about politics, business, and life in general. One special experience I had while travelling with him has had a profound influence on my life. It occurred in Senatobia, Mississippi, where we had gone for a district conference. We arrived about noon and were accommodated in the home of a member. President Whitaker and I shared a room on the second floor.

There were several hours before the first meeting started, so the President lay down for a nap. There was a bookcase in the room, and not being sleepy, I decided to read. At random I selected a book, which turned out to be Alexander Pope's *Essay on Man*. I was enthralled. It was the first time I had ever read at length in a book of high literary merit, other than the scriptures. It seemed to open for me a vista that until then had been closed. Since then, I have avidly read and enjoyed many of the great writers of western civilization. Each time I read one of the literary masters, I am thrilled and excited and filled with the desire to develop what inherent literary skills I may have to the maximum extent.

In retrospect, I can see why I was prompted to pray for the privilege of working closely with President William P. Whitaker. He taught me many important things at an impressionable period of my life which were vital for me to understand and which have been of essential value to me as my life has unfolded.

CHAPTER SEVEN

A Prophecy of My Mission President

by Francis M. Gibbons

At the time of my release from the Southern States Mission, I had a long interview with President Heber Meeks, my second mission president, with whom I had served as mission secretary. This was in the days before mission presidents had assistants among the missionaries. I had, therefore, served him in the role of an assistant and counselor but without the title. As a result, we had worked very closely together, and he had taken a fatherly interest in me. As we sat together talking, I shared with him my goal of becoming an attorney. He said that as a young man, he had a similar ambition but that he had to give it up because of a weakness in his eyes which made it impossible to spend the long hours reading, which legal study required. When I told him it would be necessary for me to work to finance my education and that I hoped it would be possible for me to obtain employment in Washington D.C. for this purpose, he suggested that while I was in Washington that I call on Edgar B. Brossard, the president of the Washington D.C. Stake and member of the U.S. Tariff Commission. I did this.

As we talked further, President Meeks made the promise or prediction that if I were honest in my profession and remained faithful to the doctrines of the Church that I would ultimately "sit in the leading councils of the Church." From April 1970 to April 1986 when I served as the secretary to the First Presidency, I, indeed, sat in the leading councils of the Church. I regularly attended the meetings of the First Presidency, the weekly meetings of the Council of the First Presidency and Quorum of the Twelve, and the monthly meetings of all general authorities. During the first part of my tenure, I also attended the weekly meetings of the First Presidency and the Presiding Bishopric. And on an annual basis during this time, I attended the meeting of the Council on the Disposition of the Tithes, which included the First Presidency, the Twelve and the Presiding Bishopric. Because of all this, I had almost come to believe that President Meeks' prophecy had been fulfilled because he had said only that I would "sit" in these councils, not that I would be a member of them. My call to the Seventy in April 1986 cast a new light on what my mission president told me.

During the intervening years, President Meeks and I stayed in contact with each other. After his release from the mission he managed the Church ranch in Deer Park, Florida, which is near Orlando. He encouraged me to move to Orlando to practice law, believing there was great opportunity there for me. And later when he returned to Utah, he periodically visited me in my office and a time or two consulted me about legal matters in which he had an interest. In this way, a father-son relationship was fostered, which continued up until his death, which occurred only about two weeks before my call to the Seventy. I was one of the speakers at his funeral, which was held in one of the chapels in the Salt Lake Ensign Stake. I regret that he did not live to see the fulfillment of his prediction. He was a superior man— intelligent, faithful and wise. He was a gentleman who was never thrown off balance. He had deep spirituality, serving as a sealer in the Salt Lake Temple up to the time of his death at about age ninety-five.

CHAPTER EIGHT

The Vision of Father Mason
by Daniel Bay Gibbons

As a young boy, Wilford Woodruff was instructed in the principles of the gospel by a neighbor, an aged man named Robert Mason. Though he claimed no authority, "Father" Mason, as he was known in the neighborhood, believed that the church and kingdom of the Lord would soon be restored to the earth. During Wilford's last visit to the old man in 1830, Father Mason prophesied that Wilford would soon see the restoration of the kingdom, and that Wilford would live to become "a conspicuous actor" in that kingdom.

Wilford Woodruff was born March 1, 1807, near Farmington, Connecticut, to a religious and hardworking family. As a boy, Wilford and his brother Azmon often assisted their father, who was a miller. At his father's mill, he discovered one of his great joys in life as his father taught him to catch fish in the millstream, which ran cool and deep beside the mill where they worked. He enjoyed this sport for the remainder of his life, and took time to fish wherever he was, whether in the mission field in Great Britain or traveling on the plains with the saints en route to the Great Basin. This was truly a fitting pastime for a man destined to become one of this dispensation's great "fishers of men."

From his earliest years, it seemed as though some malevolent force had especially marked Wilford for destruction. He later reported that on twenty-seven separate occasions his life had been spared. At age three, he fell into a cauldron of scalding water; later, he fell from a beam inside a barn onto the bare floor; he fell down stairs and broke one of his arms; he very narrowly missed being gored by a bull; he was almost smothered by a full load of hay; he barely escaped drowning; he nearly froze to death; he was bitten by a mad dog; he fell from a porch and broke his other arm; he was poisoned; he split the instep of his foot open with an ax; while climbing an elm tree, he fell about fifteen feet to the ground and was knocked unconscious; he fell from a horse and dislocated his ankles and broke his leg in two places. By the time he reached manhood, he had broken nearly every bone in his body and narrowly escaped death many times. Wilford believed that these misfortunes could be attributed to a destructive power that sought to thwart his life's mission. Many times he testified that it was God's mercy and protecting care that had preserved him.

Even as a boy, Wilford exhibited a remarkable spirituality. He was a profound student of the scriptures, and attended as many church meetings as he could, particularly among the Presbyterians. However, he felt something lacking in the preaching of the professional ministers. One of the great experiences of Wilford Woodruff's youth was his friendship with an aged man in the neighborhood named Robert Mason, who instilled in young Wilford the principles of fasting, prayer, and the reality of the gifts of the Spirit. Of his association with Father Mason, Wilford later wrote:

> In the days of my youth I was taught by an aged man named Robert Mason, who lived in Sainsbury, Connecticut. By many he was called a prophet; to my knowledge, many of his prophecies have been fulfilled. The sick were healed by him through the laying on of hands in the name of Jesus Christ, and devils were cast out. His son was a raving maniac. After praying and fasting for him nine days, he arose on the ninth day and commanded in the name of Jesus Christ the devil to come out of him. The devil obeyed and the boy was made whole from that very hour. This man instilled these principles into my mind as well as into the mind of my oldest brother Azmon.

Father Mason did not claim that he had any authority to officiate in the ordinances of the gospel, nor did he believe that such authority existed on the earth. He did believe, however, that it was the privilege of any man who had faith in God to fast and pray for the healing of the sick by the laying on of hands. He believed it his right and the right of every honest hearted man or woman to receive light and knowledge, visions, and revelations by the prayer of faith. He told me that the day was near when the Lord would establish His Church and Kingdom upon the earth with all its ancient gifts and blessings. He said that such a work would commence upon the earth before he died, but that he would not live to partake of its blessings. He said that I should live to do so, and that I should become a conspicuous actor in that kingdom.

The last time I ever saw him he related to me the following vision which he had in his field in open day: "I was carried away in a vision and found myself in the midst of a vast orchard of fruit trees. I became hungry and wandered through this vast orchard searching for fruit to eat, but I found none. While I stood in amazement finding no fruit in the midst of so many trees, they began to fall to the ground as if torn up by a whirlwind. They continued to fall until there was not a tree standing in the whole orchard. I immediately saw thereafter shoots springing up from the roots and forming themselves into young and beautiful trees. These budded, blossomed, and brought forth fruit which ripened and was the most beautiful to look upon of anything my eyes had ever beheld. I stretched forth my hand and plucked some of the fruit. I gazed upon it with delight; but when I was about to eat of it, the vision closed and I did not taste the fruit."

"At the close of the vision I bowed down in humble prayer and asked the Lord to show me the meaning of the vision. Then the voice of the Lord came to me saying: 'Son of man, thou hast sought me diligently to know the truth concerning my Church and Kingdom among men. This is to show you that my Church is not organized among men in the generation to which you belong; but in the days of your children the Church and Kingdom of God shall be made manifest with all the gifts and the blessings enjoyed by the Saints in past ages. You shall live to be made acquainted with it, but shall not partake of its blessings before you depart this life. You will be blest of the Lord after death because you have followed the dictation of my Spirit in this life.'"

When Father Mason had finished relating the vision and its interpretation, he said, calling me by my Christian name: "Wilford, I shall never partake of this fruit in the flesh, but you will and you will become a conspicuous actor in the new kingdom." He then turned and left me. These were the last words he ever spoke to me upon the earth. To me this was a very striking circumstance. I had passed many days during a period of twenty years with this old Father Mason. He had never mentioned this vision to me before. On this occasion he said he felt impelled by the Spirit of the Lord to relate it to me.

The vision was given to him about the year 1800. He related it to me in 1830, the spring in which the Church was organized. Three years later when I was baptized into the Church of Jesus Christ of Latter-day Saints, almost the first person I thought of was this prophet, Robert Mason. Upon my arrival in Missouri with Zion's Camp, I wrote him a long letter in which I informed him that I had found the true gospel with all its blessings; that the authority of the Church of Christ had been restored to the earth as he had told me it would be; that I had received the ordinances of baptism and the laying on of hands; that I knew for myself that God had established through Joseph Smith, the Prophet, the Church of Christ upon the earth.

He received my letter with great joy and had it read over to him many times. He handled it as he had handled the fruit in the vision. He was very aged and soon died without having the privilege of receiving the ordinances of the gospel at the hands of an elder of the Church.

The first opportunity I had after the truth of baptism for the dead was revealed, I went forth and was baptized for him in the temple font at Nauvoo. He was a good man, a true prophet; for his prophecies have been fulfilled. There was so much reason in the teachings of this man, and such harmony between them and the prophecies and teachings of Christ and of the apostles and prophets of old, that I believed in them with all my heart. (Matthias F. Cowley, *Wilford Woodruff—His Life and Labors*, pp. 16–18)

Wilford subsequently fulfilled Father Mason's prophecy by becoming one of the most "conspicuous actors" in the kingdom. He became one of the mightiest missionaries of this dispensation, serving extended missions to the

Southern States, to the Eastern States, and to Great Britain. In 1839, he was ordained an Apostle and lived a lifetime of faithful service to the Church. In 1889, at the age of 82, he became the fourth President of the Church.

CHAPTER NINE

"A Rowdy Irish Lad"

by Francis M. Gibbons

The missionary who baptized Charles A. Callis, apologetic about his lack of proselyting success, reported that his only convert was "a rowdy Irish lad" who lived with his widowed mother in Liverpool, England. This obscure boy from Dublin, Ireland, who lacked an extended church family or influential friends, spent much of his life as a missionary for The Church of Jesus Christ of Latter-day Saints and rose to become a member of the Quorum of Twelve Apostles. The numerous people converted by Charles A. Callis, or through his influence, represent a shadow army of Latter-day Saints whose Church memberships trace directly to that missionary in Liverpool who thought he had failed.

Charles A. Callis was born in Dublin, Ireland, on May 4, 1865. His father died soon after his birth, and Charles and his widowed mother moved to Liverpool, England. There he met missionaries of the Church and was baptized. After immigrating to the United States, Charles Callis spent his growing up years in Summit County, Utah. His first mission was to Wyoming, which was then part of the Summit Stake. Later he was called to the British Mission, where he served as the president of the Irish Conference. A few years after their marriage, Charles and his wife, Grace Pack Callis, were called as missionaries to the Southern States and were first assigned to labor in Jacksonville, Florida, where Charles was the conference president. Later he presided over the South Carolina Conference; and in August 1908, while still in South Carolina, he was called to succeed Benjamin E. Rich as the president of the Southern States Mission with headquarters in Atlanta, Georgia. This was the beginning of a twenty-five-year period of concentrated Church service, during which he presided over all of the members of the Church in the states of Florida, Georgia, Mississippi, Alabama, and South Carolina. He also was responsible to direct the work of the missionaries throughout this vast area. These responsibilities were complicated by the fact that there were no stakes in this entire area, so that he alone was ultimately responsible for all aspects of the work in the five southern states. This entailed abandoning his law practice and foregoing any political plans he may have had. Before he and Grace were called to the South, Elder Callis had successively served as the constable in Coalville, Utah; a member of the Coalville City Council; a representative to the Utah Legislature; the city attorney of Coalville; and the county attorney of Summit County.

Because he served in the South so long, and because he had such vast Church authority, Charles A. Callis became a venerable father figure to all members living there. Boys named Callis proliferated among Mormon families. Leaders and members came to expect and to gratefully receive directions from the President, even in the most detailed aspects of their Church assignments or their personal affairs. While staying in a Latter-day Saint home, for instance, the President never felt restrained in counseling the woman of the house about her cooking, her housekeeping, her laundry or her personal appearance. And the priesthood leaders could expect to receive explicit instructions about their work. All this was done without rancor or any sense of carping criticism, but merely in the spirit of a benign parent who was anxious for the Church to succeed and for its members to act and to look like true Latter-day Saints who aspired to become like their Heavenly Father.

President Callis was especially strict with the missionaries. He ran a very tight ship and wanted it made known he was in charge and that things would be done his way. Three examples will suffice, shared by his missionaries who were my personal friends:

Delbert L. Stapley, later a member of the Twelve, arrived in the South after World War I, where he had served in the Marine Corps. At his first meeting with President Callis, he arose to walk across the room to get a hymnbook. "Where are you going Elder?" the President demanded. "To get that hymnbook," he answered. "Sit down, Elder; the missionaries in this mission don't need hymnbooks." Elder Stapley's rigid training in the Marine Corps helped him to brush this off easily. What happened the next day at first caused him to wonder about his president. Elder Stapley and a companion were going to their field of labor in company with President Callis. Their vehicle was a horse drawn buggy. After the gear was loaded, the President instructed the other elder to drive while he rode in the passenger's seat. To Elder Stapley he said, "You walk." By then Elder Stapley was truly irritated and had unpleasant thoughts about his mission president. After a mile, however, Brother Callis dismounted and said to Elder Stapley, "Now you ride." Then the president walked two miles. With a tear in his eye, Elder Stapley reported, "I have loved him ever since."

When William P. Whitaker and his wife arrived in the South, President Callis assigned them to Jacksonville, Florida. The Whitakers had leased their home in Pocatello, Idaho, and depended on the rent to help keep them in the field. When their renter defaulted in payment, Elder Whitaker approached President Callis during a district conference to request permission to go home to straighten out his finances. Looking up at the tall elder who towered over him by almost a foot, President Callis said, "Did you come out here to fill a mission?" "Yes I did," answered the elder. "Then fill it," said President Callis, who turned and walked away. Elder Whitaker, who later became president of the Southern States Mission, reported that everything worked out all right.

Elder Heber Meeks was the president of the Alabama Conference under President Callis. While in Montgomery, Alabama, he received a wire from the President instructing him to go to Birmingham, Alabama, far to the north to conduct the funeral service for a prominent member who had passed away. Since Elder Meeks had a severe cold and had two missionaries laboring near Birmingham, he wired President Callis to suggest the two elders conduct the service. He received a curt wire in answer, which merely said, "You go." As Elder Meeks rode north on the train, he fumed over the incident, wishing he would die or get deathly sick just to show the President. "But darn it, I got better," he reported. Elder Meeks also later became the president of the Southern States Mission.

The love and loyalty these three men had for President Charles A. Callis were feelings uniformly shared by all who served under him.

Elder Callis was assigned to create the first stake of the Church in the South at Jacksonville, Florida, in January 1947. He was very excited about it, seemingly looking on the event as a capstone to his career. His companion was Elder Harold B. Lee of the Twelve. Elder Callis declined to stay in the luxurious home of A. O. Jenkins and his wife in Jacksonville, preferring to stay in the small apartment connected with the chapel so that he could "be with Grace," who had passed away. They often had stayed there together. When the conference was over, Elder Lee and Mission President Heber Meeks drove south toward Miami to attend some meetings. Elder Callis had remained in Jacksonville and was being driven to an appointment by Brother Jenkins. When the Apostle fell silent in the car, Brother Jenkins found he was unconscious. He never revived. Alerted by the highway patrol that there was a message in Jacksonville for Elder Lee, he learned of the passing of his friend. Elder Lee later conducted funeral services for Elder Callis in Jacksonville then accompanied the body home, where services were also held in Salt Lake City. A great sense of peace permeated the proceedings, where family and associates paid their respects to the rowdy Irish lad who had become a truly great man.

CHAPTER TEN

"Tragedy was His First Companion"

by Daniel Bay Gibbons

The Deseret Evening News for February 10, 1896 contains an article with a dateline of "Dresden, Germany" entitled: "Elder Ott's Death and Burial, His Fellow Elders Lay His Body to Rest in Dresden." The article tells the sad tale of the death and burial Elder Joseph Alma Ott, the first missionary ever called from the small town of Tropic, Utah. Elder Ott died a few days after arriving in Germany, without ever learning German, bearing his testimony or preaching a sermon. His influence, however, was far from over, and is a testimony of how the Lord brings great things to pass from small beginnings.

In October of 1895, twenty-four-year-old Joseph Alma Ott of Tropic, Utah, married Elizabeth Jolley in the St. George Temple. The Ott family had only moved to Tropic three years earlier, accepting with several other families, including the Jolleys, the call of President Wilford Woodruff to settle the area. The new couple returned to Tropic after the wedding, and settled down to a happy life. Then, three weeks after the wedding, their lives were turned upside down by yet another call from the prophet. This time the young husband was called on a full-time mission to Germany. It was not uncommon in those days to call married men to leave their family for a period of years to serve foreign missions.

Heedful of the call, Elder Ott left immediately for Salt Lake City, where he was ordained a Seventy and set apart as a missionary to Germany by Elder Abraham H. Cannon, a member of the Quorum of the Twelve. He booked passage on a sailing ship for Europe and arrived in the port city of Hamburg, Germany, in January of 1896.

"Unfortunately," a family member wrote, "tragedy was Elder Ott's first companion." While stepping from the ship onto the dock in Hamburg, he slipped and fell into the cold water of the harbor. He was rescued from the icy waters and traveled on to his first assignment in Dresden, but swiftly became ill with diphtheria. After an illness of twelve days, he died and was buried in Dresden, Germany, the city of his first and only assignment in the mission field. His companions wrote:

> Though not able to speak the German language, having been here but a short time, yet Brother Ott was filled with the spirit of his mission and was hopeful and happy. His Master called him to another sphere of action. The messenger of death was diphtheria, to which he succumbed after an illness of some twelve days. With tender care and brotherly affection was he nursed by Brothers McEwan and Weller, who remained by his side day and night.

The Elders wrote of the simple funeral services, held in St. Paul's cemetery in Dresden with only the missionaries and a few members present.

> Thus was laid away our faithful and beloved brother in this far-off foreign land, one grave among thousands of others, one more servant of the Lord who has given his life for his Master and the Gospel. . . . We filled up the grave ourselves. While shoveling the soil, a human skull, pieces of clothing and the remains of a coffin were encountered. The inspector informed us that these were the remains of a person buried twenty-two years ago. So the ashes of one helps to cover the ashes of another. . . . We mourn not for the departed, but our hearts go out in love and condolence for the bereaved wife and family. . . . May the young wife who said farewell

to her husband forever on this earth, after a marriage of three weeks, be comforted. . . . Although the occasion which brought the Elders here to Dresden was a sad one, yet it was a pleasure to have so many Utah "boys" together at one time and we enjoyed each other's presence very much. It made us feel that we were not so far from home after all. (Deseret Morning News, January 24, 1890.)

A white marble tombstone was placed over the grave of the fallen missionary. Paid for by donations of the local members and missionaries, it stood 1.6 meters high and read:

In Memory of the Missionary of the Church of Jesus Christ of Latter-day Saints, Joseph A. Ott, Born Dec. 12, 1870, Virgin City, Utah, Died Jan. 10, 1896 in Dresden. Dedicated to Him by His Fellow Believers.

The widow and family of Elder Ott grieved back home in Tropic. The local members sent a photograph of this tombstone to Elder Ott's family, where for many years it was displayed in the home of his parents. The Church offered to bring his remains back home to Utah, but the family decided to leave his body in Germany, the place the Lord had called him to labor.

And so, the story appeared to be over. A young missionary had died. But the influence of Elder Ott was only beginning.

In 1908, a woman named Maria Strauch was walking through the St. Paul's Cemetery in Dresden after tending the grave of a relative, when she had a remarkable experience. It was a cloudy day, but she saw a pillar of sunlight shining on a single tombstone in the cemetery. Going to investigate, she saw that it was the grave of Elder Ott. She read the inscription and felt that this was a message to her from heaven. She read the name of the Church and decided to find it. After much searching, she found the tiny branch of the Church in Dresden. Within a year, she and her husband, Hermann, and most of their thirteen children were baptized. The Strauch descendants provided great strength for the Church for generations to come.

CHAPTER ELEVEN

Prayer Atop the Temple Walls
by Francis M. Gibbons

One night David King Udall, a young married man about to embark on a mission *to England, climbed up the unfinished walls of the Salt Lake Temple, and under the stars of heaven poured out his heart to God. He asked for guidance on his mission and protection for his new bride in his absence. In return, he solemnly covenanted to devote the remainder of his days in the service of God. Over the course of his long life he lived up to this covenant in a remarkable way.*

David Udall and Eliza King Udall were baptized into The Church of Jesus Christ of Latter-day Saints in their native England. Several months later, they immigrated to the United States with a company of Mormon converts, which arrived at New Orleans, Louisiana, in late 1850, after a nauseous two-month voyage from Liverpool, England. A seven-day boat trip up the Mississippi brought them to St. Louis, Missouri. There David found employment at a brick yard, where he worked for several months to earn money for the remaining trip to Salt Lake City. While the couple was in St. Louis, their first child, David King Udall, was born on September 7, 1851. A year later, the Udall family arrived in Salt Lake City, Utah. Persuaded by a newfound friend, Benjamin F. Johnson, they moved south to Salt Creek, later called Nephi, Utah.

Young David grew up on his father's farm, where arduous labor in the fields hardened his muscles, gave him an appreciation for the worth of work, and created an empathy for those who made their livelihood from hard physical labor. Living with convert parents also awakened his innate spirituality and confirmed his convictions about the divine origins of the Church. His spirituality was reinforced when his deceased sister, Emily, a special friend, appeared to him one day near the family home.

David King's faith in the church was tested when he received a call to fill a mission in England only a few days after his marriage to Eliza Luella (Ella) Stewart. There was no hesitancy in accepting the call. The depth of his convictions about the Church was shown in Salt Lake City while he was preparing to leave for England. One night he climbed to the top of the unfinished temple walls, and there in the moonlight he poured out his heart to his Heavenly Father. He asked for guidance in fulfilling his mission, prayed for Ella's protection in his absence, and sought wisdom in raising his children. In turn he covenanted he would dedicate the rest of his life to God's service and would do all in his power to rear his children to love and serve Him. Looking back at the end of his long life, we see how this volunteer covenant was fulfilled in a remarkable way.

Elder Udall served faithfully in England. He was a thorough and effective missionary, whose ardent testimony imbued his converts with confidence and conviction. While there, he developed a close rapport with his mission president, Elder Joseph F. Smith of the Quorum of the Twelve Apostles. Ever after, Elder Smith "kept his eye" on David King Udall, in whom he saw a natural leader who would be a potent force in building the young church.

In 1880, David King Udall was called as the first bishop of the ward in St. Johns, Arizona. This was on the frontier of the church. Life there was raw and unsophisticated. Earlier Church leaders had contracted to purchase a town site from Jewish merchants, the Barth Brothers, west of an existing Mexican village. The purchase price was in cattle. Soon after arriving in St. Johns, Bishop Udall and two associates travelled to Utah to get help from the Church in completing the purchase. Bishop Udall was given an order, signed by President John Taylor, to receive 450 head of cattle from the Church herd near Kanab, Utah. These were driven to St. Johns, across the frozen Colorado River, and turned over to the Barth Brothers. The bishop and two assistants then surveyed the tract, laying out sites for homes, churches, and civic facilities. Despite much opposition from the old settlers, the new Mormon community survived and grew by dint of hard labor and many fervent fastings and prayers.

Meanwhile, Bishop Udall had taken a second wife, Ida Hunt, daughter of John Hunt, bishop of the nearby Snowflake Ward. Being a leading Mormon polygamist in the area, Bishop Udall was the target of federal officials who sought to charge him under the anti-polygamy laws. Unable to obtain credible evidence of unlawful cohabitation, and still wanting to harass him, these officials charged the bishop with perjury. The charge was based on a supposed misstatement he had made under oath on a printed form in connection with the application of a friend for a land patent. Convicted on the spurious charge, despite the lack of any evidence of intention to commit a crime, he was sentenced to the Detroit Correctional Institution, where he was imprisoned for several months. He was pardoned by President Grover Cleveland, and his criminal record was expunged when the flawed nature of his conviction was exposed. In gratitude, Bishop Udall's first son born after the pardon was named Grover Cleveland Udall; and the main street in St. Johns was renamed *Cleveland Avenue.*

Bishop Udall was sustained as the first president of the St. Johns Stake in 1887. He served for thirty-five years, being released in 1922. Several years later, he was called as the first president of the Arizona Temple in Mesa, Arizona, where he served for seven years. While serving in the temple, he wrote what is thought to be a final testament to his family. In it he said, in substance, that the physical frontiers of the United States had been essentially conquered and that the frontiers of tomorrow were in the field of politics and government. The implied challenge to his family to seek to subdue these frontiers, as he had sought to conquer the physical ones, seems to have been accepted, as we see that direct descendants of David King Udall have served as judges, congressmen, mayors, a U. S. cabinet member, a U. S. presidential candidate, a city manager, and a state attorney general.

In his last months, David King Udall, an ordained patriarch, continued to give patriarchal blessings to members of his large family, which included fifteen children and numerous grandchildren. He died February 18, 1938, full of years and conspicuous achievements. He was laid to rest in the St. Johns cemetery on a wind-swept bluff overlooking the little Mormon village he had been so instrumental in creating and nourishing.

Part Two

"OVER THE STORMY SEA"

It may not be on the mountain height
Or over the stormy sea,
It may not be at the battle's front
My Lord will have need of me.
But if, by a still, small voice he calls
To paths that I do not know,
I'll answer, dear Lord, with my hand in thine:
I'll go where you want me to go.

—Hymn 270, Verse 1

CHAPTER TWELVE

The Barber from Serbia

by Daniel Bay Gibbons

I n 1934 an elderly Salt Lake City barber of Serbian ancestry died in humble circumstances. Found among his few belongings was a short personal history, written in imperfect English, which chronicled one of the most remarkable lives of missionary service ever offered by a Latter-day Saint. Warned in a dream as a young man, Mischa Markow abandoned a pilgrimage to the Holy Land in 1887, and embarked on another, greater pilgrimage: membership in The Church of Jesus Christ of Latter-day Saints, a pilgrimage which ultimately led him to preach the restored gospel in eight nations.

Mischa Markow was born October 21, 1854, in Hungary to Serbian parents. Growing up in a religious home, Mischa developed a keen spiritual sensitivity. Mischa became a barber. In his early thirties he felt a keen desire to visit the Holy Land on a personal pilgrimage. After traveling extensively and visiting the sites associated with the life of the Savior in Palestine, he took up residence in Alexandria, on the Nile delta. There he opened a barbershop.

In early 1887, Mischa had a dream of the night, which changed the entire course of his life. In the dream he was "warned" to sell his business and board the next available ship to Constantinople. Heeding the dream, he sold his business and all of his personal belongings and sought passage to

Constantinople. Like Lehi, he didn't know exactly how he would arrive at his destination, but he had an implicit faith that the hand of the Lord was guiding him. Ultimately he found a place on a ship sailing out of the port city of Jaffa in Palestine. On board ship, he soon met a fellow passenger, Jacob Spori, a missionary of the Church. Because Elder Spori was the only missionary of the Church within many hundreds of miles, the meeting of these two men on the deck of a ship in the Mediterranean was truly miraculous. Gifted in languages, Mischa was able to converse in German with Elder Spori, and throughout the voyage they discussed the restored gospel as the ship plied north over the wine-dark waters of the Mediterranean. Soon after arriving in Constantinople, Mischa was baptized and ordained to the priesthood.

During his first few months in the Church, Mischa was repeatedly counseled to gather with the saints in Utah, but he expressed his great desire to first preach the gospel in Europe. Soon after his baptism, Mischa returned to his native Hungary and then commenced to travel through Europe, preaching the gospel as he had opportunity. He spoke several languages and was a powerful speaker. His travels took him to Belgium, where he found a ready audience for his teaching. It is likely that he was the first person to preach the gospel in Belgium. In Antwerp, he met and baptized six members of the Easelman family and others. Soon he wrote to the Church's missionary authorities in Germany and requested that missionaries be sent to Belgium. Soon thereafter a branch of the Church was organized in Antwerp, comprised initially of members Mischa had converted.

In 1892, Mischa immigrated to the United States and settled in Salt Lake City. His rest from missionary labor was short lived, however. On April 21, 1899, he was formally called and set apart as a missionary to labor in the Balkan lands of southeastern Europe.

Returning to Europe, Mischa first served in Serbia, but was arrested and banished by the local authorities. Leaving Serbia, he returned to his native Hungary. There, he and his companion, Elder Hyrum M. Lau, ultimately baptized thirty-one persons in Tamesvar, Hungary, over a period of about four months, and organized a branch of the Church there, prior to being banished from Hungary.

Dejected following his banishment from Hungary, Mischa reported to the president of the Turkish Mission in Constantinople, and was counseled to go to Romania, where he found many souls ready for the gospel. On February 27, 1900, he wrote from Bucharest: "With the help of God I have now baptized seven persons, one a Romanian [sic], one Bulgarian, one Greek, and four Saxon sisters . . . during all that time, I was very much afraid, I feared that they would expel me from Roumania, and I became very much concerned about the welfare of those faithful souls." [sic] Notwithstanding, or perhaps in spite of, his success in baptizing a few converts in Romania, Mischa was again driven out of the country, and completed his mission in Munich, Germany. He arrived home in Utah on August 28, 1901.

This time Mischa's rest from his missionary labors was even briefer, as he was called on yet another mission to Europe in 1903. During this mission, he was assigned by Elder Francis M. Lyman, a member of the Twelve living in Liverpool, England, to go to Russia to preach the gospel. Mischa registered himself with the district court in Riga, Latvia, on October 3, 1903, and commenced to teach among the Germans living in Riga. Mischa later baptized three families in Riga.

One of the unique things about Mischa's missionary service was the fact that he frequently traveled and preached alone. He once wrote to a friend, "It is very difficult to labor in a strange land." Though he was undoubtedly beset with loneliness and fear for his safety, he treated his labors with the same zeal with which he approached his pilgrimage to the Holy Land as a young man.

Following his last mission, Mischa returned to Salt Lake City, where he worked the rest of his life as a barber. He died on January 19, 1934. Among his possessions was a personal history, written in a sweet but imperfect English, which contained this summary of his extraordinary missionary service:

I, Mischa Markow Preach the Gospel in 8th Kingdoms: 1. Belgien, 2. Hungary, 3. Romanien, 4. Bulgarien, 5. Germany, 6. Turkey, 7. Russia, Serbia. I was 11 th times in to City court. 4th Times in to Magistrate, 2. Times in to High Cort. I was 3 Times guardet Police stud by the Gate and if somebody wants to come to hear me police did not Let him in. And that was in Romanien, Bulgarien, & Serbien. 2 Times I was banished that is in Hungary and in Serbien. I was 2 times in the jail in Romanien and Hungary.

CHAPTER THIRTEEN

"The Mormons Will Never Find Us"

by Francis M. Gibbons

Auguste Lippelt's husband, displeased with the baptism of his wife and children in Bremen, Germany, moved his family to Brazil, where they settled in a sparsely populated area in the interior. There he is reported to have said, "The Mormons will never find us here." The following account dramatically demonstrates how the Lord inspires his servants to feel after and locate His saints, no matter where they live. It also proves that great things often proceed out of that which is small. So it was with Auguste Lippelt, one of the true pioneers of the Church in South America.

Sister Auguste Kuhlmann Lippelt, who was married to Robert Frederick Heinrich Lippelt, was the mother of seven children. Her fourth child, Robert, named after his father, became very ill. On a certain Tuesday in 1920, Robert told his mother and his sister, Auguste, "Today in this room, I saw my deceased grandparents, who said that I would die on Thursday but that they were my hope." The son said the grandparents told him the true church of Jesus Christ was on the earth and they could find it by going to a certain place in Bremen. The son died as prophesied on Thursday, nine days later.

When Auguste and several of her children went to the place identified by Robert, they met Sister Demmel, who was a member of The Church of Jesus Christ of Latter-day Saints. On her invitation, they later attended a meeting in the Bremen branch of the Church. This began a period of intense study and prayer for the mother, Auguste Lippelt, during which she gained a firm testimony that the Church is true. The older Lippelt children shared that conviction and, with their mother, were anxious to join the Church. When the husband was consulted about this, however, he adamantly opposed it, as he had heard negative reports about the Church. Still, the mother and her children continued to study the literature they had received and, when possible, to attend Church meetings. Periodically Auguste pleaded with her husband to relent and to allow her and the children to be baptized. He refused to yield until one day, mellow from a few draughts of good German schnapps, he announced, with alcoholic flair, she could do anything she wanted. Before Robert could change his mind, Auguste gathered the children together and went to the branch president who arranged for the Lippelts to be baptized in the Weser River.

The husband was not pleased, although he did nothing to annul the baptisms. He did, however, decide to move his family away from the influence of the Church. Learning that Brazil offered land subsidies to immigrants, Robert Lippelt booked passage to Porto Alegre for himself and family in September 1923. Sailing down the Weser River past Bremerhaven and into the North Sea, their ship navigated to the Atlantic for the long nauseous voyage to Porto Alegre in Southern Brazil, not far from the border with Uruguay. Moving inland by train and wagon, the family arrived at a remote area first called Princess Isabel, but later named Ipomeia. Robert Lippelt, viewing the family's stark isolation, except for a few scattered German farmers, is reported to have said, "The Mormons will never find us here."

But Robert did not reckon with the faith and persistence of his wife, Auguste. Later she wrote a letter to the President of the Church, Heber J. Grant, asking for materials to help in teaching her children. This letter was referred to Rheinhold Stoof, president of the recently created South America

Mission with headquarters in Buenos Aires, Argentina. In time, President Stoof travelled to Ipomeia, Brazil, by ship, train and horseback to visit Sister Lippelt and to appraise the possibility of assigning missionaries to the area. Arriving there while Robert Lippelt was away, the President held a cottage meeting in the Lippelt home, to which the German-speaking neighbors were invited. This is thought to be one of the first meetings of the Church held in Brazil.

This visit convinced President Stoof there were good opportunities to proselytize in the area, and soon missionaries began to work among the German-speaking people. The first two missionaries assigned to work there were Fred Heinz and Emil Schindler. This set the pattern for proselytizing in Brazil for many years, with missionary work being limited to the German-speaking population. Only later did the Mormon missionaries begin to work among those who spoke Portuguese.

With Mormon missionaries working in the area and with their harvest of converts adding strength to the Church, life for Auguste Lippelt took on a much rosier hue. The one dark spot in her life was the failure of her husband to embrace the gospel. However, after Auguste's death and after an illness had crippled him, Robert Lippelt began to read *The Book of Mormon* and to study other Mormon literature. He told his daughter, Georgine Lippelt Blind, with whom he was living in Ipomeia, "I want to go where my wife is. I want to be baptized." He later told the missionaries, "If you will carry me into the Peixe River and baptize me, I will walk by myself again." He was carried in a chair to the bank of the river and was baptized. His faith was rewarded so that he regained the ability to walk.

The numerous progeny of Robert and Auguste Lippelt, inspired by the example of faith shown by their ancestors, continue to play vital roles in the growth of the Church in Brazil. Georgine Lippelt Blind, for instance, a daughter who immigrated to Brazil from Bremen, Germany, with her parents when she was a young girl, has filled several missions as a worker in the Sao Paulo Temple.

CHAPTER FOURTEEN

16,000-Mile Journey
by Daniel Bay Gibbons

W hen *Heber C. Kimball arrived in Manchester in 1837 to preach the gospel, he hoped that the message would spread quickly throughout England. However, even he was amazed at the speed with which the work of conversion progressed in the Potteries region of England, and then how the work extended from England into Europe and even to the uttermost reaches of the vast British Empire. The taking of the gospel to Australia in 1840 by a seventeen-year-old elder, William James Barrett, is really a continuation of a chain of conversions commenced in England.*

The seed, which ultimately sprouted into a vibrant Australian arm of the Church, was first planted in the Potteries region of England. The key event was the 1839 conversion of a sixteen-year-old boy by the name of William James Barrett. The Potteries were a cluster of large and small towns situated in Staffordshire, England, and were so named because the area was then the center of Great Britain's earthenware manufacturing industry. It was in this part of the country that Heber C. Kimball, Wilford Woodruff and others found an exceptionally fruitful field for the preaching of the gospel in the late 1830's.

William James Barrett was born January 25, 1823, in Burslem, Staffordshire, England. Shortly before William encountered the Mormon missionaries, his father had died and his mother had quickly remarried. He was an earnest and intelligent young man, and judged by later events, a natural born preacher. He was also a bold and independent soul, based on the fact that he was the only member of his family to join the Church. He was baptized sometime in late 1839 in Staffordshire, probably by William Clayton and Alfred Cordon. Though still a boy, he quickly attracted the attention of the leaders of the Church in England. On July 9, 1840, Alfred Cordon recorded in his journal:

> after I had been Preaching at Hanley bro Wm. Barratt came to our house and told me that he expected he was going to South Australia he was about seventeen years of age he had a mother and a stepfather he was to have started on the Saturday The Spirit made it manifest to me that if he went he must be ordained to the Office of an Elder.

Elder George Albert Smith also wrote that he had received the same strong spiritual impression that the young man should be ordained, and indeed had traveled from Manchester to the Potteries to heed that prompting. These two seasoned leaders soon ordained the young man to the office of Elder in the Melchizedek Priesthood, supplied him with books, instructed him in his duties as an elder and a minister of the gospel, counseled him to write to the Prophet Joseph Smith, and sent him on his way to Australia, a journey of some 16,000 miles.

En route to Australia, the young missionary wrote to Elder Cardon and reported the progress of his journey. He asked his friend to: "give my love to all the Saints and tell them that as many as are faithful I will meet them in Zion bringing my Sheaves with me." Upon his arrival in Australia, William also wrote to the Prophet reporting the slow progress of his teachings. This is the last communication sent by William to the leaders of the Church. Eventually William fell away from the Church, but not before finding and baptizing a man named Robert Beauchamp.

Beauchamp was a member of a religious group called Plymouth Brethren. The Lord often moves in a mysterious way, for notwithstanding the disaffection of William Barrett, Robert Beauchamp, his first and only convert, was to become the true founding father of the Church in Australia, and one of the longest serving presidents of the Australasian Mission.

Twenty-five years later, Robert Beauchamp sent a letter to President Brigham Young recounting his conversion by William Barrett in 1841. He reported that he found William "amiable and intelligent," and possessed with a remarkable command of the scriptures. After becoming convinced of the truth of the work, Beauchamp submitted himself to baptism under the hands of the young elder. He then reported: "I enjoyed the society of this young elder for about three months, when business called him into the country, and I never saw him more."

CHAPTER FIFTEEN

"One of a City, Two of a Family"

by Francis M. Gibbons

eremiah's prophecy that the latter-day gathering of Israel would occur "one of a city and two of a family" applies with compelling impact to Charles W. Penrose. Frequently converts to the Church must leave behind father, mother, sisters and brothers to embrace the true faith. This was true with Charles after his baptism, as he left not only his native England, but his family as well. However, the Lord blessed him for his sacrifice, and he served the Church and his fellow men with great distinction as a missionary, writer, journalist and finally as an Apostle and member of the First Presidency.

Charles William Penrose, who was born February 4, 1832, in London, England, was the only member of his father's family to join The Church of Jesus Christ of Latter-day Saints. He was baptized May 14, 1850, only three months after his eighteenth birthday. His joy of embracing the true gospel and kingdom of God was tempered by the knowledge that he must soon bid farewell to a family that had no sympathy for his newfound faith. This is a common dilemma of the chosen, who often find themselves joining the Church "one of a city and two of a family." (Jeremiah 3:14)

Within two months of his baptism, Charles was called as a missionary for the Church. During a period of ten years, he was instrumental in converting many, as he helped to raise up branches in Maldon, Danbury, Chelmsford, and Colchester. During this ministry, he also exhibited the gift of healing to a remarkable degree, began to hone his administrative skills as president of the London Conference, and gave hints of latent literary skills, as he wrote articles for the *Millennial Star* and composed lyrics for hymns.

Elder Penrose immigrated to the United States in 1861, settling with his family in Farmington, Utah. There, and in Cache Valley, Utah, where he moved in 1864, he farmed and taught school. A call to the British Mission in 1865 interrupted his farming career, one for which he was ill suited due to his urban upbringing in populous London. He never returned to it. Back in England, he served successively as president of the Essex and the London Conferences, travelled extensively throughout the country and was assistant editor of the *Millennial Star* under Elder Franklin D. Richards of the Twelve.

After a brief try as a shopkeeper, Elder Penrose was introduced to his permanent vocation when Elder Franklin D. Richards invited him to edit the *Ogden Junction*, a newly formed newspaper. After a year, he became editor-in-chief and business manager. Meanwhile, he became a member of the Weber Stake High Council, a member of the Ogden City Council, a member of the Territorial Legislature and a delegate to the 1872 constitutional convention.

The reputation Charles W. Penrose forged in Ogden prompted President Brigham Young to invite him to join the staff of the *Deseret News* in June 1877, a few weeks before the Prophet's death. By September 1880, Elder Penrose had become the editor-in-chief. His service with the *Deseret News* was interrupted in 1885 when he was called on a brief mission to the States and then on another mission to Great Britain. In England he served under mission president, Daniel H. Wells, travelling extensively with him, serving as president of the London Conference, and acting again as assistant editor of the *Millennial Star*. Returning to the United States, he resumed his work as editor of the *Deseret News* while spending time in the eastern United States over a two-year period, working behind the scenes in the interests of statehood for Utah. During this period, Elder Penrose, who was engaged in plural marriage, was sought by officials on federal indictments under the Edmunds Act. He was relieved of this harassment when President Grover Cleveland granted him full amnesty.

For several years, beginning in October 1892, while the *Deseret News* was under lease to President George Q. Cannon, Elder Penrose worked as the editor-in-chief of the *Salt Lake Herald*. Then in 1896 he was sustained as an assistant church historian. Meanwhile, when the lease of the *Deseret News* ended in 1899, President Lorenzo Snow appointed Elder Penrose editor-in-chief.

Throughout his years with the *Deseret News* and *Salt Lake Herald*, Elder Penrose was active in the Church, in politics, and in personal writing projects. He became a counselor in the Salt Lake Stake Presidency, serving under President Angus M. Cannon; was a member of the Territorial Legislature and of the Constitutional Convention; and he authored a series of twelve tracts titled *Rays of Living Light,* which were extensively used throughout the Church for many years. He also wrote many articles for Church and other publications.

On July 7, 1904, Elder Penrose was called as a member of the Quorum of the Twelve Apostles to fill the vacancy created by the death of Elder Abraham O. Woodruff. Two years later he was called to preside over the European Mission, succeeding Elder Heber J. Grant. He returned from Europe in 1910, and a year later he was called as second counselor to President Joseph F. Smith, succeeding President John Henry Smith. When President Joseph F. Smith died in November 1918, Brother Penrose became second counselor to President Heber J. Grant; and in 1921 he became the first counselor to President Grant, succeeding President Anthon H. Lund. He served in that capacity until his death on May 15, 1925.

President Penrose's literary legacy still lives among us through lyrics he wrote for Latter-day Saint hymns which are sung regularly in Church meetings around the world, which include, "O Ye Mountains High," "God of Our Fathers We Come Unto Thee," and "School Thy Feelings."

CHAPTER SIXTEEN

"Work Done in Secret"

by Francis M. Gibbons

I n the months following the American Civil War, one Parson Smith, an American Baptist minister, emigrated from the United States to Brazil. Little did Parson Smith know, but his relocation to South America would prepare the way for his great-granddaughter, Roberta McKnight Hunt, to receive the restored gospel, and then to translate the Doctrine and Covenants into Portuguese. While her work of translation was performed anonymously and in secret, the scriptural promise to her was that the Lord would reward her openly.

Following the end of the Civil War in the United States, almost ten thousand Americans from the South migrated to Brazil. There the emperor, Dom Pedro II, offered land subsidies to the immigrants to help develop the country's vast agricultural resources. Many of these immigrants settled in or near a community appropriately called Americana located not far from Sao Paulo, Brazil.

These newcomers not only brought their agrarian skills with them, but also their Protestant faiths, their southern culture, and their English language. So when schools were established among them, the children of these immigrants were taught Portuguese, the national language, while from infancy they learned English, which was the language of the home. Thus, the children who emerged from these immigrant families, and their descendants, grew up bilingual, equally adept in both languages. While this bi-lingual skill was helpful to all who possessed it, it was to have special significance and uses in the life of Roberta MacKnight Hunt who was born in Americana, Brazil.

Roberta was the great-granddaughter of "Parson Thomas," an expatriate Baptist minister. From her infancy, she showed special language aptitude and skill. When she had completed her initial training at the local schools, she enrolled at the University in Sao Paulo, from which she graduated in linguistics.

While she attended the University in Sao Paulo, Roberta underwent significant changes in her religious thinking. Because the Baptist church she normally would have attended was some distance from her dormitory, she began to attend other Protestant churches that were nearby, including a Methodist church and a Presbyterian church. It was the first time she had attended churches other than her own, and she was surprised and troubled by what she found. It was especially bewildering to her that each of these churches, as well as her own church, professed to be the one true church. Since their doctrines disagreed, it was obvious they could not all be right. Faced with such perplexity, what was one to do? Roberta later thought it providential that at this time there came into her hands the pamphlet "Joseph Smith Tells His Own Story," published by The Church of Jesus Christ of Latter-day Saints. She read it avidly because Joseph Smith's dilemma was mirrored in her own experiences. And she adopted the solution young Joseph eventually employed by going to the Lord in fervent prayer. This, coupled with assistance rendered by two Mormon missionaries who were working in the area, resulted in her conversion to The Church of Jesus Christ of Latter-day Saints. She was baptized on April 10, 1943, by Elder Richard Benjamin Platte in the River Tiete, which encircles Sao Paulo.

Roberta MacKnight's enthusiasm for her newfound religion and her testimony about the answers she had received to her fervent prayers had a serious effect upon her family and others residing in Americana. Most of her family ultimately joined the Church. And fully half of the then-living descendants of the Reverend Elijah Quillin, who first took the Baptist religion to Brazil, became Latter-day Saints.

In time, Roberta was married and sealed in the United States to Jay B. Hunt, a former missionary from the Brazilian Mission whom she had met in Sao Paulo. When Jay received orders to go overseas with his air force unit, Roberta went to live with his parents in Salina, Utah. There she taught school while awaiting the birth of her first child, who was born in October 1945. Meanwhile, events unknown to her were coalescing which would lead Roberta MacKnight Hunt along a road she had never expected to travel, while using the superior linguistic skills she had acquired in Brazil.

The surprise development came in a communication from Rulon S. Howells, a former Brazilian mission president, who said he had been authorized to invite her to translate the *Doctrine and Covenants* into Portuguese. She accepted this daunting task willingly, but with much trepidation after being set apart to the task. So that she would have privacy and quiet, she rented a small apartment near the home of her parents-in-law in Salina and began the tedious work. The last pages of her first draft were mailed to Elder Lloyd Hicken in Bountiful, Utah, on May 16, 1946, a week before her husband was discharged from the Air Force. Elder Hicken had been engaged to type the manuscript in final form.

There then followed a long series of meetings to edit and to proofread the manuscript before publication. Roberta participated in all these, supported by her husband, Jay, who adjusted his school and work schedules to accommodate the demands on his wife's time. When Rulon S. Howells was called to serve again as the mission president in Brazil, he took the final, corrected manuscript with him. There, an index and notes were completed, and the book was copyrighted and printed in Brazil. Later in 1950, President Howells sent Roberta the first printed copy of the *Doctrine and Covenants* in Portuguese. A cover letter thanked and congratulated her and, paraphrasing 3 Nephi 13:4, said that though the translator's name did not appear in the book, "the work which had been done in secret, would be rewarded openly by the Lord."

This was reward enough for Roberta Hunt, whose accident of birth in Brazil of a people with American roots provided her with the bi-lingual capacity to perform this significant work.

CHAPTER SEVENTEEN

Bringing the Gospel Home to Korea

by Daniel Bay Gibbons

t has been said that any organization is merely the lengthened shadow of one man. Applying this maxim to the founding and growth of the Church in Korea, the figure of one man, Kim Ho Jik, looms very large, indeed. Prior to 1951 there was not a single Korean national who was a member of the Church. Kim Jo Hik joined the Church while pursuing graduate studies in the United States at Cornell University. Upon his return to Korea, he soon was named to a cabinet level position in the South Korean government. Because of his political prominence, Kim Ho Jik was in a unique position to influence and accelerate the growth of the Church in Korea.

Born on April 16, 1905, in what is now North Korea, Kim Ho Jik demonstrated his great intellectual powers very early in life. As a teenager, he moved to South Korea to pursue his education in the finest schools available. He graduated from Suwon Advanced Agricultural and Forestry School at age nineteen, and then was awarded a bachelor's degree in biology from Tohoku University in Japan in 1930. Back in Korea, he quickly rose to positions of great influence in the Korean government. He became a university president and later the director of the Suwon Agricultural Experimentation Station. His research focused on ways to improve the diet, nutrition, and quality of life for Koreans. In this capacity, his work came to the attention of the highest government leaders in South Korea.

In his personal life, Kim Ho Jik was a deeply spiritual man. Born into a family that practiced Confucianism, he later studied Ch'ondogyo, then Buddhism, and ultimately Christianity. He eventually joined the Presbyterian Church. He was a dedicated husband and father. He had a deep and abiding faith in Jesus Christ and His teachings.

In 1949 the president of South Korea, Syngman Rhee, arranged for Kim Ho Jik to travel to the United States to pursue advanced studies in nutritional science at Cornell University in New York. At Cornell University he received his master and doctoral degrees and became close friends with a Latter-day Saint graduate student named Oliver Wayman. Eventually Kim Ho Jik began reading literature about the Church given to him by Brother Wayman, and he began attending meetings.

On Brother Wayman's last day at the University, he felt compelled to seek out Kim Ho Jik, and he bore a moving testimony that the Lord had led him to America in order that he might receive the gospel. Further, he testified that the Lord wanted Kim Ho Jik to "take it back to his people in preparation for a great missionary work to be done there." Finally, Brother Wayman cautioned Kim Ho Jik that "if he refused to do the work the Lord had for him, another would be raised up in his place."

This testimony was really the turning point of Kim Ho Jik's life. He soon received all of the discussions from the missionaries and was baptized on July 29, 1951. At Kim Ho Jik's request, the ordinance took place in the Susquehanna River near the same location where Joseph Smith and Oliver Cowdery were baptized. As Kim Ho Jik was drawn out of the waters of the river, he heard an audible voice saying, "Feed my sheep, feed my sheep." Within a few weeks of his baptism Kim Ho Jik finished his studies at Cornell and returned to Korea.

Back in Korea, Kim Ho Jik quickly spread the gospel among native Koreans. He held weekly cottage meetings at his home, and by 1952 baptisms were occurring in ever-increasing numbers. Kim Ho Jik also rose quickly in positions of great responsibility. He became, in turn, Dean of the College of Animal Husbandry at Konkuk University, President of Hong Ik College, Chief Korean Representative to UNESCO, chairman of the Seoul Board of Education, and then Vice Minister of Education for the government of South Korea. Because of his direct influence, the Church was incorporated in Korea, paving the way for the dedication of the land of Korea for the preaching of the gospel by President Joseph Fielding Smith in 1955. The first full-time missionaries arrived in the nation in 1956.

In the early 1950's Kim Ho Jik had served as a branch president and then became the first district president in South Korea. He frequently went out of his way to teach the gospel and to cast a favorable light upon the Church. Once he was invited to address a nationwide television audience to discuss biology. Instead, he spent nearly his entire ten-minute allotment of time discussing the Church. On another occasion, the president of South Korea sent for him on a Sunday to discuss an urgent matter. Kim Ho Jik was at the branch meeting rooms teaching a Sunday School class. Kim Ho Jik refused to attend to the president's summons until he had finished his Sunday School lesson.

In 1956, Kim Ho Jik resigned his government post and, like Alma in the Book of Mormon, dedicated the remainder of his life to the building up of the kingdom. During the coming months he translated Church literature into Korean. He died unexpectedly of a stroke on August 31, 1959.

Though he was a member of the Church for only eight years before his untimely death, Kim Ho Jik left a legacy of faith and dedication almost unparalleled in the history of the Church in any nation. Because he sat in the highest councils of the South Korean government, the Lord was able to use his influence to accelerate the spreading of the gospel among the Korean people.

CHAPTER EIGHTEEN

The Boy From India

by Daniel Bay Gibbons

Unexplained spiritual yearnings led Dr. Edwin Dharmaraju, a respected entomologist, from his native India to the Samoan Islands. In Samoa, Edwin soon discovered the reason behind his spiritual promptings, as he and his wife were approached and baptized by missionaries of The Church of Jesus Christ of Latter-day Saints. One of their assignments in the Church was to return home to preach in India, where they soon established a branch in Hyderabad. Their conversion also led to the translation of The Book of Mormon *into Telegu by Sister Dharmaraju's father, a Baptist minister.*

Edwin Dharmaraju was born on May 2, 1925, in Andhra Pradesh, India. Edwin was raised in a small village where strong traditions of morality and family ties were held sacred. When he was a young man, his parents arranged for his future marriage to his wife, Elsie, who lived in the same village. Elsie came from a highly educated family, and her father, the Reverend P. Sreenivasam, was a Baptist minister. Edwin shared Elsie's Christian upbringing. Though Edwin's own family came from more humble surroundings, he endeavored early in his engagement to obtain as much education as he could. By the time of their marriage in 1950, Edwin had already received a Bachelor of Science degree from the University of Madras and had aspirations to continue his training in the field of entomology. He eventually earned a master's degree in Bapatla, India, and a doctorate degree from Kansas State University in 1968.

During the years when Edwin was alone pursuing his doctoral studies in Kansas, he frequently attended church in a Protestant congregation. One Sunday he saw a very unusual looking chapel and decided on an impulse to attend. Inside he found an LDS sacrament meeting in progress and left several hours later with a copy of *The Book of Mormon*. Though he never again attended an LDS meeting in Kansas, he did read *The Book of Mormon* from cover to cover while living in the United States.

Back in India, Edwin became a professor of entomology at the Andhra Pradesh Agricultural University in Hyderabad. Life was good for Edwin and Elsie, who by now had several children. However, Edwin commenced to feel deep spiritual yearnings, which he often communicated with Elsie. Eventually he felt inexplicably drawn toward the Pacific islands. In 1974 he heard of a position in Apia, Western Samoa, for a crop protection expert. Edwin and Elsie prayed for guidance and felt a powerful impression that they should go to Samoa.

Two weeks after Edwin, Elsie, and their three daughters arrived in Samoa, two missionaries knocked on their door, and within three months the entire family was baptized, including an older son who flew to Samoa for the baptism.

After tasting the sweetness of the gospel, Edwin's first thought, like Enos and Lehi, was toward his extended family. His anxiety for them was so great that he wrote to Church headquarters to request that missionaries be sent to India. The unexpected response was a mission call from the prophet for Edwin and Elsie to serve in Hyderabad, India! Edwin and Elsie were set apart on October 22, 1978, and Edwin was given authority to preach, baptize, ordain, and organize units of the Church in India. Within two months of their arrival in India, they had baptized twenty-two members and organized a branch in Hyderabad.

Soon after the completion of their mission, Edwin and Elsie began pondering the task of seeking out someone who could translate *The Book of Mormon* into Telegu, one of the major languages of India spoken by some fifty million people. Surprisingly, they found the translator in Elsie's father, Reverend Sreenivasam. Though he never joined the Church, he found great value in *The Book of Mormon* and undertook the task of translating a page a day at the age of eighty-two. Two years later he was finished, and Edwin and Elsie were able to present a seven-hundred-page manuscript to LDS Church President Spencer W. Kimball.

In their later years, Edwin and Elsie lived in the Gilbert Islands, where Edwin served as a branch president. Edwin's parishioners lovingly called him "President Doctor Edwin."

He died suddenly on July 28, 1985, while conferring with his counselors at the branch meetinghouse.

CHAPTER NINETEEN

The Consequences of One Conversion

by Francis M. Gibbons

What are the consequences in time and eternity of the conversion of a single man to the principles of the everlasting gospel? The answer cannot be better exemplified than in the life of Miles Romney. Baptized in the River Ribble at Preston, England, in September 1839, Miles lived a life of service to the kingdom and instilled the gospel message powerfully in the minds and hearts of his large family. By 1998 there were more than five thousand of his descendants who had become members of The Church of Jesus Christ of Latter-day Saints. Among these were men and women who have distinguished themselves in the fields of science, government, politics, business, literature, religion, the arts, athletics, education, architecture, and the professions. Among his descendants are President Marion G. Romney; George Romney, former governor of the State of Michigan; and Mitt Romney, a major U. S. Presidential candidate in 2008 and 2012. Most important, his descendants have, by and large, remained faithful to the principles of the religion that Miles Romney embraced when he was baptized in 1839.

Miles Park Romney was born July 15, 1806, in Dalton-in-Furness, Lancashire, England. He later married Elizabeth Gaskell, and the couple lived in Preston, England. The introduction of Miles and Elizabeth Romney to the religion which transformed their lives and the lives of their family occurred in 1837, when they heard a Mormon missionary, Orson Hyde, preach at a street meeting in the Preston marketplace. What the missionary said was so provocative, that they undertook a study of the doctrines of the Church he represented. This led them also to attend many meetings of the Mormon missionaries, held at the famous Cock Pit in Preston. After two years of study, and after receiving spiritual confirmation that it was the thing to do, Miles and Elizabeth were baptized in the River Ribble in Preston. Immediately they took an active interest in the affairs of the Church in their area. Meetings were regularly held in their home, and they were active in trying to interest others in the Church that meant so much to them.

When the Romneys heard about the call of the Prophet Joseph Smith for the Saints to gather to the land of Zion in the United States, they immediately began to make plans to leave their home and to migrate. They packed their personal things, including Miles' valuable carpentry tools, and boarded the ship *Sheffield* in Liverpool, England, on February 7, 1841. After fifty-one days at sea, they landed at New Orleans, Louisiana, whence they embarked on a Mississippi River steamer destined for Nauvoo, Illinois. Miles was so sick when he arrived that he needed help to disembark.

There was a feverish building boom in Nauvoo at the time. People with the building skills Miles Romney possessed were much in demand. Thus when he recovered from his long voyage, Miles Romney began to work at various building jobs in the city. He devoted much time to work on the Nauvoo Temple. It was the beginning of his dedicated labors to help build some of the most important and sacred buildings in the early history of the Church, including the Salt Lake Temple, the St. George Temple, and the St. George Tabernacle.

After the saints were driven from Nauvoo, Miles Romney spent several years working in Iowa and Missouri to save enough money to gather with the saints in Salt Lake City. The family travelled west with the Edward Hunter Company, arriving on October 13, 1850. Because of his building skills, Miles was appointed foreman of the public workshop located on the temple block. In this position he supervised the laying of the first foundation of the Salt Lake Temple. In 1856 he was released from his duties on the temple block to accept a call to fill a mission in England. He arrived in Liverpool on August 7, 1856, after a voyage aboard the *New World.* During two years in his native land, he presided over the work in Manchester, Liverpool, and Preston. He left for home in April 1858, arriving on June 23.

While attending General Conference in October 1862, Miles Romney heard it announced from the stand that he had been called to Southern Utah to help build up the Mormon settlements there. Without complaint, he moved to St. George with his family, and soon after his arrival was appointed superintendent of public works. In this capacity he directed the work of constructing both the St. George Tabernacle and the St. George Temple. The beautiful circular staircase in the Tabernacle illustrates his superior skill in woodwork. It also illustrates a certain stubbornness of character which has been inherited to one degree or another by most of his descendants, a trait which no doubt accounts for many of the outstanding achievements of the clan. It happened that the top of the carefully crafted staircase was several inches higher than the level of the top floor of the building so that on reaching the top it became necessary to step down a few inches. He flatly refused to mar the symmetry of the staircase by trimming it down.

At age sixty-eight, Miles fell from a ladder, seriously fracturing an arm and a leg. The accident caused a deterioration in his health, resulting in his death on May 3, 1877, a month following the final dedication of the St. George Temple. Before the end he was heard to say, "I anticipate the change of worlds with a great deal of pleasure." He was survived by seven of his nine children, who perpetuated in their lives the principles of faith, perseverance, and loyalty that were so evident in his own.

CHAPTER TWENTY

Girl From the Outermost Isle
by Daniel Bay Gibbons

orn in the humblest of circumstances on the Island of Froya, Anna Karine Gaarden suffered the loss of her husband at a young age and made great sacrifices to preserve the lives of her young children. When she embraced the gospel, the missionaries who baptized her were required to first clear the ice away from the beach of the fjord where she was immersed. Yet, notwithstanding the adversity of her early life, she came to exert vast influence over the Latter-day Saints, not only through her own service, but also through that of her son, Elder John A. Widtsoe of the Quorum of the Twelve.

Anna Karine Gaarden seemed to have inherited from birth the rugged character of the fishermen of Froya, the Norwegian Island where she was born and raised. Called the "Outermost Island," Froya bore the brunt of the Atlantic storms that in autumn, winter, and spring beat upon its rocky coast. During the summer months, however, when the island was in sunshine twenty hours a day or more, and when its treeless surface was adorned with bright flowers, ships from many countries came through its intricate straits to trade for Norwegian herring, cod, and salmon. Anna's father was a pilot, whose skill and knowledge of the heavily indented shoreline enabled visiting vessels to maneuver safely into the harbor at Titran, Norway.

Anna, who had attractive, sharp features, was energetic and bright. She enjoyed her studies at school, especially when a handsome new teacher, John Andersen Widtsoe, came to Titran. Nine years older than his admiring student, John A. Widtsoe paid little attention to twelve-year-old Anna; that is until ten years later, when she had grown into a beautiful young woman. They were married on December 29, 1870.

Their first child, John Andreas Widtsoe, was born January 31, 1872; and after the family moved to Namsos, eighty miles north of Trondheim, their second son, Osborne J. P. Widtsoe, was born on December 12, 1877. Tragedy struck two months later on February 14, 1878, when the father died unexpectedly. After a short stay in Titran, the twenty-nine-year-old widow and her two young sons moved to Trondheim. There the family lived on a small pension Anna received from the state, earned from the husband's work as a teacher, and on the proceeds from her work as a seamstress. Although she was attractive and truly desirable, Anna Widtsoe spurned the attentions of would-be suitors and preferred to raise her sons alone. She never remarried.

A trip to a shoemaker in Trondheim changed the lives of Anna Widtsoe and her sons in ways she could not imagine. When the repaired shoes were returned, she found a Mormon tract tucked into each one. The shoemaker, Olaus Johnsen, was an ardent member of The Church of Jesus Christ of Latter-day Saints, who was anxious to share the wealth of his newfound religion. This he did even at the risk of antagonizing those customers who might take offense at receiving unwanted literature about an unpopular church. Anna, who was an avid truth seeker, read the tracts with interest. This led to discussions with Olaus, and soon to meetings with Mormon missionaries, and eventually to her baptism on April 1, 1881, by Anthon L. Skanchy. Ice at the edges of the fjord where she was baptized had to be broken before the ordinance could take place. Although the water was icy cold, Anna said she had never felt warmer or more comfortable.

Shunned by friends, deprived of her government pension, and being anxious to enjoy the full blessings of the Church, the young widow decided to gather with the saints in America. Using her meager savings and helped by the emigration fund, Anna and her sons travelled to Liverpool, England, where they joined a group of converts from Denmark, Norway, Sweden, and England. Crossing the Atlantic on the *SS Wisconsin*, the group arrived in New York on November 7, 1883. Soon after, the Widtsoes reached Logan, Utah, where they were welcomed by Norwegian converts and former Norwegian missionaries.

Struggling with a new language, new customs, and old economic problems, the young widow and her sons settled into a new life in the Cache Valley of northern Utah. Anna soon resumed sewing for a living, and for a while operated a sewing school. She was active in the organizations of the Church and fervent in observing its teachings, especially that of regular heartfelt prayer. The dedication of the Logan Temple the year after she arrived in the valley was a time of great spiritual fervor for her. About this time, during a ward testimony meeting, Anna spoke in an unknown tongue. Another sister at the meeting gave an interpretation.

Being determined to keep the commandments with exactness, she one day burned the tea and coffee she had in her pantry, thereby giving up a habit she had enjoyed for many years. She was loyal to the leaders of the Church and would not allow any negative discussion about them in her home. Two ward teachers learned this to their embarrassment when Anna asked them to leave her home when they spoke disparagingly of an action taken by the presiding brethren. They were told not to return until they were prepared to teach the gospel and to act like God's representatives. And she corrected a convert immigrant who complained about policies of the brethren saying, "We came here to build up Zion, not to tear it down."

Fiercely independent, Anna stubbornly refused charity, except when it came in answer to prayer. Once when the mother put the last piece of wood into the stove, she called her sons to join in prayer to ask God for fuel to keep them warm. Not long after the prayer ended, a Brother Larsen, who lived down the street and with whom Sister Widtsoe was not well acquainted, knocked on the door. He was carrying a sack of coal, which he gave to the family. It was a powerful lesson the sons never forgot, that God is near and is anxious to bless those who, in their extremity, seek Him in fervent prayer.

Anna was determined these two sons would follow in the footsteps of their father. This required higher education, something not every Latter-day Saint of that day could afford. But this widow who was living at the edge of poverty could afford it. She mortgaged her home and gave any surplus income to help them. This, added to scholarships and help from kindly benefactors, enabled John to graduate from Harvard University and Osborne to graduate from the university at Logan, where he was the valedictorian. These credentials were vital later to enable John to become the president of Utah State University at Logan and then of the University of Utah and for Osborne to become the president of the Latter-day Saint College in Salt Lake and later to serve on the faculty at the University of Utah. John A. Widtsoe, of course, later became a member of the Quorum of the Twelve Apostles.

In May 1903, Anna and her sister, Petroline, were called as missionaries to Norway. They served effectively for over four years. They were able to change the attitudes of many of their former acquaintances and to lead many toward the Church. And their example was a great incentive to the younger missionaries, who marveled at their strength of character and dedication to the gospel.

To the end of her days, Anna declared that the most glorious thing that came into her life was the message left by the shoemaker. She died on July 11, 1919. Funeral services were held in the Nineteenth Ward in Salt Lake City, where the concluding speaker was President Heber J. Grant, who had been her mission president in Europe, and who extolled her virtues of faith, perseverance, and dedication to her family and to the Church. Nothing the prophet said or could have said was more impressive than a bare recital of the salient facts of her remarkable life.

CHAPTER TWENTY-ONE

Maori Forerunner
by Daniel Bay Gibbons

Old Testament prophets who foresaw the Restoration predicted that our age would be one of great spiritual outpourings: *"And it shall come to pass afterward, [that] I will pour out my spirit upon all flesh; and your sons and your daughters shall prophesy, your old men shall dream dreams, your young men shall see visions:" Joel 3:28. This prophecy was fulfilled in part in New Zealand in the 1800's, as five separate tribal priests of the native Maori people prophesied to their people that the true church of God would soon come to New Zealand. Best known of these prophecies was the one given to Paora Potangaroa in 1881. A forerunner in every sense of the word, Paora Potangaroa prepared the way spiritually for tens of thousands of his people to join the Church.*

The Church was originally established in New Zealand in 1854 among European immigrants, but not among the native Maori people. The Maori were a deeply religious people, many of whom had been converted to the Catholic, Methodist, and Presbyterian faiths. However, by the early 1880's there was great concern among the leaders of the Maori people that the introduction of Christianity among them was tending to divide them. The leaders began to question which of all of the churches was the right one for the Maori people. A great convention was held in early 1881 to consider this question. After lengthy discussion, no solution could be found. At this point the tribal leaders turned to Paora Potangaroa, who was an elderly and venerated tohunga, or tribal priest, among the Maori.

Paora Potangaroa went to his home to ponder the question, and to fast and pray for an answer. After three days of searching, he returned to the people and said: "My friends, the church for the Maori people has not yet come among us. You will recognize it when it comes. Its missionaries will travel in pairs. They will come from the rising sun. They will visit with us in our homes. They will learn our language and teach us the gospel in our own tongue. When they pray, they will raise their right hands."

The prophecy went on to state that the Maori people were some of the lost sheep of the House of Israel, and that they would learn of "Shiloh, the king of peace" and of "the sacred church with a large wall surrounding it."

As a result of this and other similar prophecies, the Maori people joined the Church in large numbers when the Church was finally preached to the Maori people. By 1884, Elders Alma Greenwood and Ira Hinckley, Jr., had baptized several hundred converts and organized thirteen branches. Paora Potangaroa's prophecies had truly prepared the way for the preaching of the gospel in New Zealand. Eventually tens of thousands of Maoris would join the Church.

CHAPTER TWENTY-TWO

From Basketball to Baptism

by Daniel Bay Gibbons

I
n 1996, the late Kresimir Cosic was inducted into the Basketball Hall of Fame in
Springfield, Massachusetts, only the third international player ever to be so
honored. Winner of four Olympic silver and gold medals, Cosic was a national
sports hero in his native land, and finally a deputy ambassador from Croatia to the
United States at the time of his untimely death in 1995. However, for Kresimir the
most significant moment of his life was always his baptism into The Church of
Jesus Christ of Latter-day Saints, performed by Hugh Nibley in 1971. For him, his
baptism and membership in the Church was the beginning of "a permanent
relationship with the Spirit."

Kresimir Cosic was born in 1948 in Zagreb, Croatia, in the former
Yugoslavia. He spent his boyhood in the city of Zadar on the Adriatic Sea. It
quickly became clear that young Kresimir had prodigious basketball talents.
The 6-foot 11-inch center began his unparalleled basketball career at the age
of sixteen, when he led his local team to its first of five national
championships. He went on to lead several Olympic teams to win silver
medals in 1964 and 1968, and a gold medal in 1980. He also later coached
another team to an Olympic silver medal in 1988.

In 1969, at the age of twenty-one, Kresimir arrived in Provo, Utah, to
attend Brigham Young University. On the basketball floor, he was the star

player for the Cougars from 1970 through 1973, leading his team to the NCAA Tournament Regionals two years in a row, and earning numerous national and conference awards. He set school records for high scorer and rebounder, was selected to the all-WAC First Team for three consecutive years, was named the WAC Most Valuable Player, and was named to the all-Decade WAC Team. He also played on three National All-Star teams.

While his storied basketball career was unfolding at BYU, Kresimir's life was taking an unexpected turn as he was exposed for the first time to members of The Church of Jesus Christ of Latter-day Saints. Not all of his experiences with members of the Church were good at BYU. He was able to observe, over a long period of time, that many members of the Church did not fully live their religion. But, after two years in Utah, he became converted to the teachings of the Church and was baptized. Especially instrumental in his teaching and conversion was Brother Hugh Nibley, the renowned scholar. Shortly before his baptism, Kresimir told Brother Nibley, "There are a hundred reasons why I shouldn't join this Church and only one reason why I should, because it's true." (Nibley, Hugh W. Teachings of the Book of Mormon: FARMS, 1993, page 36). Kresimir was baptized by Hugh Nibley in 1971. Regarding his membership in the Church, he later commented:

> The only organization I ever joined in my life was the Church. . . . Being a member of the Church does not just give you an occasional boost. It is the permanent relationship with the Spirit that teaches you—not just when the hard times come, when you are facing a war, but every day. I try to live the best I can to maintain this relationship.

After leaving BYU, Kresimir turned down offers to play professional basketball in the NBA with the Los Angeles Lakers and the Boston Celtics. Instead, he decided to return to Yugoslavia and his native Croatia to play basketball. He continued to win most valuable player (MVP) honors in his homeland and on all-European teams, and in 1980 he coached the silver-medal-winning team in the Olympics. He became a national sports figure in his native land and one of the most universally known and loved figures in the former Yugoslavia.

The decision of Kresimir Cosic to turn his back on the NBA and its financial rewards, and to return to Croatia in 1973 had far-reaching implications for the growth of the Church in the former Yugoslavia. Back home he served as a missionary and later as a district president of the then-Yugoslavian and later Croatia District. He also translated *The Book of Mormon* into his native language. He rendered crucial assistance in the establishment of the Church throughout the former Yugoslavia. In 1975, Brother Cosic worked successfully with President Neil D. Shaerrer, president of the Austria Vienna Mission, in gaining legal recognition for the Church in Slovenia. He was able to open many doors for the Church, in large part because of his status as a national sports figure.

Kresimir's celebrity in his native land frequently overshadowed that of senior Church leaders to whom he reported. Elder Russell M. Nelson has recounted a humorous incident that occurred during the Apostle's visit with Brother Cosic to high-ranking government leaders of Serbia and Croatia in 1987. Following the visit, it was reported that the officials had admitted that they weren't particularly eager to meet with Elder Nelson, but that they were thrilled to meet Kresimir Cosic, whom they watched regularly on television.

Following his glorious sports career, Cosic rendered a great public service to the newly independent Croatia by serving in the Croatian diplomatic corps. He became one of the first Croatian diplomats to the United States following the political breakup of the former Yugoslavia. As he began his diplomatic service, his nation was embroiled in a bitter and bloody civil war. However, Brother Cosic believed that *The Book of Mormon* provided both a sad parallel and a solution to his country's overwhelming internal problems. Regarding *The Book of Mormon*, he stated:

> It is the picture of the world we now live in. If there ever was a time that this world needed a prophet and the spirit of prophecy, it is today, because nobody else can make sense of the things that are going on. How

can people live together for many years and then within a few months, for no right reason whatsoever, end up in a cruel war?" (LDS Church News, 1/9/93).

It was while he was serving as Croatia's Deputy Ambassador to the United States that he died in Washington D.C. on May 25, 1995, after a year-long battle with non-Hodgkins lymphoma. He was only 46 at the time of his death.

CHAPTER TWENTY-THREE

The Long Voyage of a Chinese Orphan

by Daniel Bay Gibbons

n 1857 a British merchant vessel docked for a few days at the mouth of a river on the coast of China. When the ship weighed anchor and returned to sea a few days later, on board was a new passenger — a three-year-old Chinese boy. Some twenty years later, this boy, now a man, settled in Western Samoa. Using his sailor's wages, he purchased the plot of ground where a future temple would stand, and he became one of the great benefactors and pioneers of the Church in the South Pacific.

In about 1854 a boy was born in China and was likely orphaned at a young age. Three years later, in about 1857, the little boy was befriended by British merchant sailors, as their ship lay docked at the mouth of a Chinese river near where the boy lived. When the ship returned to sea a few days later, the little boy was on board. Named "Ah Mu" by the sailors, perhaps a corruption of the name of the river where he was found, the boy grew up on board British merchant ships. Plucked from the land of his birth while still almost in infancy, Ah Mu now began a long voyage toward his divinely appointed destiny. He was to remain as a crewmember on board British ships for some twenty years, obtaining his "education" from his weather-beaten companions and from the sea itself.

Then, one day when Ah Mu was in his twenties, he left the seafaring life behind him for good and went ashore for the last time in Western Samoa. He was a free man, unlike many other Asians on the Pacific Islands, and a British subject. Using a small amount of money he had accumulated during his years as a sailor, he purchased a beautiful plot of land in Vaimoso and built himself a handsome two-story home. He later married a beautiful Samoan woman, and they had a family.

In Samoa, Ah Mu and his family became practicing Christians and associated themselves with the London Missionary Society. One Saturday Ah Mu sent his oldest son with a basket of food for their pastor. The boy returned home to report that the pastor had angrily refused the offering, saying that it was not enough. Ah Mu observed to his family, "Oh, he can't be a man of God to do a thing like that." (Percy John Rivers, *Autobiography of Percy John Rivers*, Edited by Jennie Hart (1992), p. 12.) A short time later, Ah Mu met missionaries of The Church of Jesus Christ of Latter-day Saints, and he and his family members were baptized on February 21, 1897.

In his few remaining years Ah Mu was one of the great supports to the Church in Western Samoa. He provided both food and shelter for the missionaries and allowed his home and land to be used as a gathering place for the Saints. His land became known as Pesega, or "place of singing." In 1902, Ah Mu donated his land to the Church in exchange for the payment of one dollar. This became the Church's headquarters in Western Samoa. Eventually the mission headquarters, a chapel and later a stake center, the missionary training center, the Church College of Western Samoa and the Apia Samoa Temple were all built on the land given by Ah Mu to the Church.

Ah Mu died on August 5, 1910, at the age of 56.

Part Three

"AT THE BATTLE'S FRONT"

It may not be on the mountain height
Or over the stormy sea,
It may not be at the battle's front
My Lord will have need of me.
But if, by a still, small voice he calls
To paths that I do not know,
I'll answer, dear Lord, with my hand in thine:
I'll go where you want me to go.

—Hymn 270, Verse 1

CHAPTER TWENTY-FOUR

The Sole Survivor
by Daniel Bay Gibbons

E merging from the terrors of World War II, the sole survivor of his German battle unit, his life hanging by a thread, Hans-Juergen Saager felt an overriding Providence which protected him and beckoned him on toward a "special purpose" for his life. Hans-Juergen found that "special purpose" when he later encountered the Mormon missionaries and commenced a new life of service, including his call to serve as the first West German citizen to preside as a full-time mission president.

Hans-Juergen Saager was born February 26, 1925, in the city of Stetin, then a part of Germany and now located in Poland. His father was a printer and found it necessary to move his family to Hamburg in 1927 to pay off some family debts. Hans-Juergen was only two years old when the family moved to Hamburg, and there he spent his formative years in a happy and loving home. Eventually Hans-Juergen studied in a trade school and apprenticed in an electrical wholesale business. His future looked bright. The only shadow over his life was the start of World War II. In 1943 he was conscripted into the German army at the age of 17, and thus began a sixteen-year nightmare of war, pain, injury, and illness, which shattered his peaceful life.

Hans-Juergen suffered grave injuries in the war, and almost didn't live to see its traumatic conclusion in May of 1945. Hans-Juergen was the sole survivor of his original company who lived to see the end of the war. On several occasions he survived while his companions around him fell. It was during the terrible heat of battle that he commenced to feel that God had saved his life for a "special purpose," which Hans-Juergen did not yet know. As the war wound to its horrific conclusion, he continued to feel that the Lord was protecting him from death. He was in the last jeep to retreat across one of the last operating bridges on the Rhine River as the German army fell back in disarray before the advancing Allied forces. Commencing in May of 1945, he was imprisoned under American military jurisdiction, spending much of the time hospitalized for treatment of his extensive injuries. Although imprisoned for a full year, he bore little animosity toward his American captors. Indeed, he later developed a special bond with Americans, including hundreds of full-time missionaries who served under his loving leadership. Ironically, he spent part of his imprisonment in Duesseldorf, the city where he later served as president of the Germany Duesseldorf Mission.

When not hospitalized, Hans-Juergen was assigned by his American captors to write out discharge papers for German soldiers who lived within 50 kilometers of the place of their incarceration. Since he lived a great distance from the prisoner of war camp, he was in the last group of soldiers discharged. He spent the final months of captivity in France, and was finally released in May 1946, a full year after the cessation of hostilities.

Though he was discharged and returned to his hometown of Hamburg, the war was not yet over for Hans-Juergen. Because of the gravity of his injuries, he was again hospitalized. From May of 1946 until 1959 he was in and out of hospitals and was unable to pursue his schooling or work because of his disability. During this period he also saw nearly all of his companions pass away from injuries in the hospital, and Hans-Juergen was once again left to question what "special purpose" God had in mind for him in the future.

Two events represented a break in the clouds for Hans-Juergen during the years of his painful treatment and slow recovery. The first was his marriage in 1953 to Irmgard Will in Hamburg, and the second was his meeting of LDS missionaries in 1957. Hans-Juergen has written that the first thing he learned from the missionaries was how to pray. Prayer soon brought deep solace and comfort to Hans-Juergen in the midst of his physical afflictions. Still gravely ill from his war injuries, Hans-Juergen made a solemn promise to the Lord that, "if He would allow me to live, I would promise to serve Him until my life on this earth finds its end." As the first step in fulfilling this personal covenant, Hans-Juergen started to teach mutual and genealogy classes in the Hamburg-Wilhelmsburg Branch, even before his baptism. Finally he and his wife were baptized on August 28, 1958.

As a new convert, Hans-Juergen's Church responsibilities soon increased dramatically. He was called as a branch president in 1960, as a bishop in 1963, and then as a stake president in 1969. As he served to the best of his physical ability, the Lord also blessed him with a miraculous physical recovery from his war injuries, so that in 1959 he was able to start working for the first time since the war. Not only was Hans-Juergen able to work again, but he also returned to trade school. Whereas the fourteen years after the end of the war had meant only pain and hospitalization for Hans-Juergen, he now experienced a great increase of health and vitality as he worked long hours to support his family and serve in the Church. He wrote, "The Lord provided me with the strength to work as I never had before, to work for Him and to work for our living." Finally, the war was over for Hans-Juergen Saager.

Hans-Juergen's wife, Irmgard, passed away in 1970. The pain of her death was lessened by the firm faith that they both had in the blessings of eternal life.

Following the death of his first wife, Hans-Juergen entered a new and exciting phase of his life, as he moved to Frankfurt to work for the Church. It was while he was living there that he married and was sealed to his second wife, Ursula Wiese, in the Swiss Temple. Ursula had been baptized in Hamburg in 1963 with other members of her family during the time that Hans-Juergen served as her bishop. During her conversion, Ursula struggled mightily with a lifetime addiction to cigarettes and coffee. However, the missionaries taught her that this and all other problems could be overcome through faith and prayer. Following their counsel, Ursula had prayed fervently for the strength to overcome. She writes: "I stopped smoking on a very beautiful Sunday morning, went to Church, brought my missionaries home for dinner, and never touched a cigarette again in my life."

Within three years of their marriage, Hans-Juergen was called as president of the Germany Duesseldorf Mission. The mission boundaries included areas where Hans-Juergen had both served in the German military and been imprisoned after the war. And here he was once again associated with many young Americans—only now they were not his military captors, but the full-time missionaries over whom he was called to preside. Though Hans-Juergen had never had children of his own, he soon became a loving and tender "father" to hundreds of young men and women who served under his direction. In his calling as mission president, and in other Church service, Hans-Juergen felt that he had finally discovered the "special purpose" for which the Lord had preserved his life.

Hans-Juergen died in Germany on June 7, 2001, at the age of seventy-six.

CHAPTER TWENTY-FIVE

"Fear Turned to Love"
by Francis M. Gibbons

Prior to World War II there were several thousand Latter-day Saints in Germany. These faithful souls were cut off from all contact with Church headquarters commencing in 1939, upon the withdrawal of all foreign missionaries from the country. At that time a young married returned missionary named Karl Herbert Klopfer was called as the mission president, with ecclesiastical responsibility for all of the saints in Germany. Unfortunately, President Klopfer was soon called into the German army himself. For the next six years, until his death in a prisoner of war camp in 1945, he attempted to minister to the needs of the scattered German saints while in a German military uniform.

Born April 11, 1911, in Werdau, Germany, Karl Herbert Klopfer and his parents were baptized into The Church of Jesus Christ of Latter-day Saints in 1923, when Karl was twelve years old. The Church soon became the center of their lives. Family prayer, gospel study, and attendance at Church meetings were the standard fare for this exemplary Mormon family. Young Karl added to the quality of family and Church gatherings with his musical skill at the organ and piano.

As Karl Klopfer grew up in Werdau, he was much influenced by the American missionaries who came and went. He was intrigued by the language spoken among them and by the mantle of authority that rested upon them. He sought to emulate these Mormon elders, both in their speech and their preaching. He undertook the study of English in school and tried to expand his usage of it by conversing in English with the missionaries. And he studied the doctrines of his adopted religion intently in the hope he could become qualified to serve in the mission field. His hope became reality in 1929 when he received a call to serve in the German Mission.

This was a period of pivotal growth for the young German convert. His knowledge of the culture and the language enabled him to teach with skill and insight. And the rigors and the ups and downs of missionary work taught him patience and perseverance. Meanwhile, assignments with missionaries from the United States enabled him to increase his proficiency in English. So adept did Elder Klopfer become in his second language, that more than once it was said of him that English seemed to be his native tongue.

Perhaps the most important by-product of Karl Klopfer's service in the German Mission was the respect for him engendered in his leaders, Presidents Tadje and Budge. They saw in him a man of devotion and skill who could be trusted. This led to assignments to translate for the Church after his mission. His competence in both English and German, his sound doctrinal understanding, and his knowledge of Church protocol superbly qualified him to serve as the translator for visiting General Authorities. In this capacity, he translated for, among others, Elder George Albert Smith and Elder John A. Widtsoe of the Twelve, and Elder Thomas E. McKay, Assistant to the Twelve, when they toured in Germany.

When the decision was made to withdraw missionaries from Europe at the beginning of World War II in 1939, the authority to direct Church affairs was given to local members. In Germany, twenty-eight-year-old Karl Herbert Klopfer was appointed as the president of the East German Mission. President Klopfer moved his family into the mission home in Berlin, which was located near the Brandenburg Gate. Soon after, President Klopfer was called into the German army. The next six years, until his death in 1945, was a time of terrible conflict in the life of Karl Klopfer and his family. A man of love and peace, he was forced by circumstances to participate in a war of dreadful severity.

Away from Berlin most of the time, he had to direct the affairs of the mission through his counselors. He was often lonely for his family and the saints, but never more so than one December near Christmas while he was stationed in Esbjerg, Denmark. A month before he had learned that the mission home in Berlin had been destroyed in a bombing raid. Although his family had escaped injury, he was distraught and saddened.

He felt impelled to seek out the local Latter-day Saints to worship with them and to seek solace from them. It was a risky thing to do, as his superiors forbad associating with locals. It could mean a court martial were he found out. But he was determined. Not knowing the location of the Esbjerg Branch chapel, Karl began humming a well-known Latter-day Saint hymn, loud enough so passersby could hear. A young girl stopped him and asked in Danish, "Mormon?" When he nodded yes, she led him to the branch chapel. As German soldiers were the enemy, Karl's arrival was greeted with apprehension. When he checked his rifle with the branch president, however, this feeling subsided. And when he rose and spoke, fear turned to love. A young Danish girl who was present later wrote of the incident: "He then gave testimony of the truthfulness of the Church. It was wonderful to see a man in the uniform we hated speak with so much love for us. He was happy to be among the Saints."

As the war wound down, Karl was transferred to the eastern front. His regiment was captured in Ukraine and he was confined in a Russian prisoner of war camp. He died there at age thirty-four. A comrade who survived later reported that Karl died of starvation. He was buried in a lonely grave in Puschke, Ukraine, near Kyiv.

CHAPTER TWENTY-SIX

Revelation at Naval Boot Camp
by Francis M. Gibbons

I received my first patriarchal blessing not long before I left for my mission to the Southern States in January, 1942. At the time there apparently was no patriarch in the Phoenix Stake, and so I was sent to the patriarch of the Maricopa Stake in Mesa, Patriarch John Nash. I drove there one night with my mother to receive my blessing. My recollection is that Mother received her blessing at the same time. When the patriarch had finished giving me my blessing, he said: "When you have finished your mission, I want you to come back for another blessing.

After returning home in February 1944, one of my high priority items was to follow up on the patriarch's request. I learned, however, that Orlando Williams was then the patriarch in Phoenix. After explaining the situation to my priesthood leaders, I was given a recommend to receive the blessing from Patriarch Williams. As I prepared to go to him, the thought uppermost in my mind was that I receive some revelatory insight about the identity of my wife. So, I prayed earnestly beforehand that the patriarch would be inspired to provide this insight.

On arriving at Brother Williams' home, I found that he had neither a secretary nor a dictating machine. Because I was skilled in shorthand, I sat at his dining room table and wrote the blessing as the patriarch gave it, standing behind with his hands on my head. It was a beautiful blessing and quite long. After some time he paused as if he were about to stop. Since he had said nothing about the thing that concerned me most, I offered a silent prayer that he would be inspired to do so. After a lengthy pause, he then continued: (I do not have the blessing before me, but I think this is the essence of it, if not a verbatim quote.) "Seek the Lord in prayer as to your companion in life, and in due time he will reveal to you the one he has reserved for you, and you will know by the promptings of the Spirit that she is to be the mother of your children. Together you will enter the House of the Lord, there to receive the ordinances of the holy priesthood which will bind you as one, that you may work together throughout the eternities, and that you may have a claim upon your children and your children's children, that you may have an endless posterity in the kingdom of our Father. You will have influence with your children and will be able to teach them in the ways of the Lord, and they will hearken unto your counsel and advice, and your testimony will have weight with them; and they will become mighty men and women in Israel and pillars of strength unto the Church, and you will rejoice in them throughout this life and throughout the eternities to come."

On receiving this blessing, I had no doubt that in due time the identity of my eternal companion would be revealed to me. Soon after, I was inducted into the U. S. Navy and was sent to San Diego, California, where I received my basic training at the Naval Boot Camp there. Afterward, I was assigned to an amphibious training base at Oceanside, California, located between San Diego and Los Angeles. We lived in Quonset huts on the beach, where we trained in making amphibious landings. I had a second-level bunk in one of these huts; and one day after receiving a cache of mail, I went there to read it in seclusion. I made myself comfortable and read slowly through the letters from home. I also found a Church section of the *Deseret News* and an *Improvement Era* (the predecessor of *The Ensign*) among my mail and had started to read those when, leafing through the *Improvement Era*, I found an article written by Helen Bay entitled "His Secret Weapon, Letters." Helen was one of the several lady missionaries whom I had met while in the mission field. I knew her no better than any of the others I had met there and had not so much as thought of her since leaving the mission field several months before. But, I had hardly begun to read the article when the words came clearly to my mind, "This is your wife," and that was accompanied by a burning in the bosom. The Lord had thus fulfilled the promise of the patriarch that the identity of my wife would be revealed to me.

With that knowledge, I was faced with difficult problems. The first was a matter of timing because the likelihood was that we would soon be sent overseas. The second was how to broach the subject to Sister Bay. At the time, I had no idea where she was serving. Furthermore, I did not know whether she was engaged to or interested in another man. Nor did I know what her attitude toward me was or would be. The logical first step in resolving these was to find out where she was. I did this by writing a letter to her addressed in care of the mission office at 485 North Avenue N. E., Atlanta, Georgia. In it I merely congratulated her on the article as coming from an acquaintance from the mission field. As a means of guaranteeing that she would respond, I mentioned the theme of her article—the need to cheer servicemen by writing to them—and indicated if she didn't respond with a letter, I would expose her to her readers as a fraud.

At the time, Helen was serving in Tallahassee, Florida. Since there was no airmail service then, my letter went by train to Atlanta and then by train to Tallahassee, which, as I recall, took about ten days. She was in no particular hurry to answer a prosaic letter from a young elder she had met and worked with briefly in the mission office, but whom she did not know well; and besides that, she was busy doing her missionary work and had precious little time to write letters, even to her family. So it was some time before she answered so as to provide me with her address. Having that, I immediately fired off a second letter, which was full of chitchat about our mutual acquaintances, missionary work, the navy, etc. Again, she was painfully slow in answering so that by the time I received her second letter I was faced with a terrible dilemma. I had, in the meantime, been assigned to the staff of Commodore Britton whose flagship was the USS Chilton, APA 38, which was scheduled to leave soon for the Far East. I did not know how long I would be gone; I still did not know about any romantic entanglements Helen was involved in, and therefore felt strongly the need to make my suit known to her before leaving. Therefore, I did something that in retrospect seems to me to be almost beyond belief. In my third letter I told her all. I tried to soften it by saying I knew it would be a great shock, that I did not expect an immediate favorable response, but that, under the circumstances, I felt the need to let her know. Her answer was what I expected. She was obviously trying to back track. So her third letter to me was reserved and between the lines said "whoa there, buster, not so fast." This was of no concern to me as I had anticipated what her response would be. I answered promptly, indicated that I was content with and understood her reaction and would accept in good grace any final answer she might give. We then continued to correspond for several weeks until sometime in late November, or thereabouts, Helen wrote to say that in reviewing her patriarchal blessing she had found some things which were significant to her and that as a result, after prayer, she had received a spiritual witness that I was to be her husband. I barely had time to con-tact my brother-in-law, Howard Elliott, to ask that he purchase a diamond ring and send it to Helen in Tallahassee, which he did. I then called her on the telephone, talked to her for fifteen or twenty minutes, and soon after left on the Chilton, destined for the Philippine Islands where we prepared for the invasion of Okinawa.

In the ensuing months, Helen and I corresponded frequently. It was a long-distance courtship during which, I believe, we became better acquainted with each other than do most couples who court in the usual way. We found that we shared the same goals and interests, were unified in our commitment to the Church, and excited by the prospect of creating our own family life and traditions. Later, when together, we found that our physical attractions for each other were equally strong, which completed the formula for a happy and exciting married life.

The Chilton and our sister amphibious transport ships carried the first U. S. assault troops to Okinawa. After landing them there, we remained in the area, providing material and munitions support and sometimes handling the overflow of wounded GI's who could not be cared for on the hospital ships. Sometime after the initial landings, Japanese soldiers began swimming out to the fleet at night with explosives taped to their bodies in an attempt to detonate their charges against the hulls of our ships. When this was discovered, a maneuver called "night retirement" was adopted. Each night, at dusk, all the ships in the fleet would weigh anchor and head for the open sea, where we would cruise all night, returning to our offshore positions the next morning after it became light. One evening as were leaving for night retirement, a squadron of Japanese kamikaze planes slipped in undetected under our radar screens and before any of us had been called to general quarters, or were aware of their presence, commenced diving into our ships. One of the kamikazes hit the Chilton a glancing blow, exploding alongside the ship, causing serious hull damage. This made it necessary for us to return to San Francisco for hull repairs. We were accompanied on the long voyage by a sister ship which was struck in the main superstructure by a kamikaze, killing many who were aboard.

While in San Francisco, I received a ten-day leave. I flew to Salt Lake City from there. I was met at the airport by Helen and her father, who drove her there because she did not have a driver's license. It was in his presence that I first embraced and fleetingly kissed the beautiful young woman who would soon become my bride.

After courting in the conventional way for two days, Helen and I were sealed in the Salt Lake Temple by Elder Nicholas G. Smith, Assistant to the Twelve, whom I had met when he visited Atlanta during my mission. Our five-day honeymoon was spent in a small apartment owned by the Steeds on West North Temple across the street north from the present Church Museum. Curiously enough, that location is just three blocks west of the site of our future home in the Canyon Road Towers.

Now we have been married for sixty-nine joyous, productive, and exciting years. The journey has been even more enjoyable and varied than either of us had dreamed. Today, I love this dear companion more tenderly than I did when she was a blooming bride. Four extraordinary children and their choice companions and eighteen grandchildren and numerous great-grandchildren have added immeasurably to our sense of joy and happiness. How we love them, every one, and we anticipate and will welcome others into the circle with equal love and joy. And how the Lord has blessed us and led us along the path, day by day. We seldom pray as a couple but that we thank the Lord for the miracle of our marriage and for guiding us in all places and at all times.

CHAPTER TWENTY-SEVEN

A Good Soldier of Jesus Christ
by Daniel Bay Gibbons

rowing up as the descendant of several generations of highly-decorated Russian and Soviet military men, Aleksandr Aleksandrovich Drachyov learned from his boyhood to fear, to respect, to despise, and to do battle against Americans. The son of a high-ranking Soviet Air Force officer, he entered the Russian Air Force Academy to train to become a fighter pilot. Then one day there was a knock at his door, and for the first time in his life, he met two young Americans face to face.

On the wall of Aleksandr Drachyov's home near Novosibirsk, Russia, hangs an elaborate family tree showing his progenitors for many generations. Flanking the family tree are photographs of ancestors on both sides of the family dressed in Russian and Soviet military uniforms. His grandfathers on both sides of the family were highly decorated officers who served in battle during World War II. His father was a high-ranking officer of the Soviet Air Force. There are few Russian families with as rich a military heritage as the Drachyov family.

Aleksandr Drachyov was born during the Cold War in the twilight years of the former Soviet Union. From his boyhood, he had one desire in life: to become a fighter pilot, like his father. He believed that true soldiers should always be ready to do battle for their families and their country. He grew up on military bases in cities that were closed to outsiders. Even as a small boy he made long flights in his father's jet, and at the age of five or six was permitted to drop his first bomb during a training run. As a young student he participated in regular air drills. Sirens would go off unexpectedly, and he and his fellow students would quickly get underground in air raid shelters. He was taught that American-made rockets could reach Russian soil within eighteen minutes.

Aleksandr had questions about religion as a boy, but growing up in a military family there was little discussion about it. He occasionally asked his parents and his grandparents about God, but they never gave him any answers. Consequently, he never read the scriptures or prayed or had any spiritual experiences in his life. He once picked up a copy of *The Bible* from a bookshelf in his parents' home and tried to read it, but it made no sense to him and he put it back on the shelf.

One night young Aleksandr had a frightening dream. In his dream, the air raid sirens were going off, and he watched as American rockets descended upon his city. As a student, he prepared himself for admission to the Russian Air Force Academy and successfully enrolled in his late teen years. There he studied aviation and military science. He also studied history and politics. He learned about the military equipment of the Soviet Union, the Warsaw Pact, NATO, and the United States. He knew what planes the United States built, and he trained to bring down those planes. In every way he was training himself to be "a good soldier," to defend against the threat of American military might. Though he had never met an American, in some ways they dominated his life, for he was preparing for the possibility of someday doing battle against them.

Then, in the years immediately after the fall of the Soviet Union, things changed for Aleksandr and his family. The threat of war against the United States and NATO decreased dramatically. The tension between the Russian military and the American military diminished. There were fewer opportunities in the Russian Air Force. Aleksandr made a significant decision to leave the Air Force Academy to pursue a life outside of the military, a step no one in his family had taken for generations. He met and fell in love with Yulia and was married, and they had a daughter, Polina.

Aleksandr and Yulia lived with little Polina in Chelyabinsk, a Russian city located on the east side of the Ural Mountains, which until about 1996 had been closed to foreigners. Aleksandr reports that in those years he was much like Amulek in *The Book of Mormon.* Like Amulek he was descended from illustrious ancestors (*See* Alma 10:3) and was "a man of no small reputation," having "many kindreds and friends." (*See* Alma 10:4). But, like Alma, Aleksandr reports, "I did harden my heart, for I was called many times and I would not hear."

Then one day there was a life-changing knock on his front door, just after he arrived home. He later pondered that his life would have been far different had he been delayed even one minute. He opened the door to find two young men, younger than himself. He said:

> They looked like children to me. They were holding blue books in their hands. I asked them what they were selling. They said they weren't selling anything, but were Americans serving as missionaries from The Church of Jesus Christ of Latter-day Saints and that they had a message for me. I had a hard time understanding them, as one of them had only been Russia for four months, and the other for six months, but I did understand that they wanted to speak to me about Jesus Christ. To that point the only other Americans I had ever seen were on the movie screen.

Aleksandr invited the missionaries inside. He was fascinated with these young men, the first two Americans he had ever met face to face. They gave him a copy of *The Book of Mormon*, and he began to read it. He said:

> I remember the first time I saw The Book of Mormon in the hands of my missionaries. It was a blue book, and they held it open in their hands so I could see. I remember the first time I took it in my hands and looked through it, turned the pages, saw the pictures, smelled the beautiful smell of the ink. It was a very important day for me.

Over a short period of time they taught him all of the missionary lessons. Aleksandr said:

I realized that these two young men were the most worthy and clean individuals I had ever met in my life. They were incredible people with an incredible message. I thought they were a little strange. For example, they didn't even drink tea or coffee, but I knew that I wanted to be with them, and we agreed to meet again and again.

I began to find answers that I had never found before. I experienced a feeling I had never felt before. I felt joy and great hope. I had peace. I saw light and something better in the future. And for the first time in my life, I prayed. After one lesson, the missionaries asked me to kneel with them to pray, but I had never knelt before in my life. They told me that I should pray about the truth of The Book of Mormon. So I began to work on myself. I knew that I could kneel down because it was before God. Then, several times when I was home, I would kneel down and begin to pray, but then heard my wife coming in from the other room, and so I would stand up. This happened a few times. So I left to go for a walk, and I found a place and knelt down and prayed. I felt that the time had come for me to be responsible for my own actions and for my own life. I felt like the time had come to look people in the eyes and not be afraid, and even to look in the eyes of my ancestors and not be ashamed of myself. It was an important moment. I had an idea that an angel would come to me. No angel came, but I had an incredibly strong feeling, and I knew that it was right. A few days later I agreed to be baptized.

When Aleksandr told his wife, Yulia, that he was going to be baptized, she said, "Okay, but let me hear this message first." She then heard all of the missionary lessons herself, and six weeks later Aleksandr and Yulia were baptized.

Aleksandr is now a seminary and institute instructor and coordinator for much of Russia. He and Yulia are the parents of six children, and Aleksandr serves as the president of the Novosibirsk Russia District. He has left behind his early dreams of becoming a pilot, to be, as Paul said, "a good soldier of Jesus Christ." (2 Timothy 2:3).

CHAPTER TWENTY-EIGHT

Relief Society President in a War Zone

by Francis M. Gibbons

erving as a district Relief Society president in the Nazi-occupied Netherlands during World War II, Getrude Lodder Zippro trusted implicitly that the Lord would protect her as she went about on her old bicycle ministering to the needs of the saints. Not only did the Lord bless and protect her, but he blessed her with a knowledge that He loves even those who wear the uniforms of the enemy.

Born in Rotterdam, Netherlands, in July 1898, Gertrude Lodder Zippro was raised in the Dutch Reformed Church. She was introduced to The Church of Jesus Christ of Latter-day Saints by her brother, Peter Lodder. At first, Gertrude and her husband showed little interest in the Mormon church. That changed following the death of their young son, who died before he had been baptized. The grieving couple could not accept the gloomy theology of their church, which condemned their beloved son to oblivion or to an eternity in hell. So when they learned that the Latter-day Saints rejected the doctrine of infant baptism and held out hope to parents like the Zippros who had lost loved ones who had not been baptized, they embarked on an intense study of the doctrines of the Mormon church. This led to their conversion and baptism. It also led to a serious reordering of their lives and to an ardent commitment to the Church and its purposes.

This commitment was to be tested in many ways. Some of the most crucial tests the Zippros faced arose out of World War II. When Germany occupied the Netherlands, strict controls over the populace were put in place: Travel was restricted, food and other commodities were rationed, and strict rules about public gatherings and religious worship were imposed and enforced. This did not hinder the Zippros in their private devotions carried on in the home, although even these were sometimes at risk because of the disposition of the occupying forces to enter private homes at will and to impose individual punishments or restrictions as they saw fit. The result was to place the family under a cloud of constant strain and fear. This was accentuated in the case of Gertrude Zippro because of her duties as the district Relief Society president. She felt a personal responsibility for the sisters in her organization and felt compelled to assist and to counsel them, despite the difficulty of transport and communication. She regularly left the home to visit sisters in outlying branches, traveling by public transport when that was available or by bicycle, if necessary. When bicycle tires wore out, replacements could not be bought because of severe rubber shortages. The problem was solved by using strips of old rubber hose in lieu of tires.

This activity was not only strenuous, it was dangerous. A woman travelling alone in a war zone was an obvious target for harassment or attack. But Gertrude did not fear. She was on the Lord's errand and had the simple faith He would protect her. And He did. She was never harmed as she went her rounds, spreading confidence and good cheer among her sisters.

There came a time when the Zippro family faced starvation. Son John Zippro remembers the fervent family prayers for food when all their stores were exhausted. One day during this period, Father Zippro, who was employed on the canal docks, saw an unmanned canal barge floating down the middle of the canal loaded with sacks of potatoes. As the barge neared the dock where Father Zippro was working, it veered at a sharp angle, coming to rest near the dock. Before the current carried the barge back into the main stream, he was able to remove two sacks of potatoes, which proved to be a godsend to the Zippro family and tided them over until other food was available. The Zippros always looked upon this incident as a direct and miraculous answer to their fervent prayers. They endeavored to make repayment for this unexpected boon by increasing their charitable efforts toward others.

Gertrude Zippro and her family found their greatest solace and joy by mingling with the saints to sing, to pray, and to bear testimony. One Sunday their branch meeting was interrupted by the entrance of two German soldiers, dressed in their uniforms and carrying side arms. The audience was fearful, not knowing what to expect. That fear increased when one of the soldiers stepped forward to speak. But his words eased their minds and taught a great lesson about the unifying effect of the gospel. He apologized for interfering with their meeting, explained he was a member of the Church and was anxious to once again partake of the sacrament, an opportunity he had missed for many months. At the end of the meeting, Gertrude and other members of the branch gathered around the two German soldiers to greet them as brothers. All animosity generated in them by the war was swallowed up in the love the gospel brings.

After the war, the Zippros immigrated to the United States where they acquired American citizenship and enjoyed the freedoms of this land and the greater blessings that the full Church program offers.

Part Four

It may not be on the mountain height
Or over the stormy sea,
It may not be at the battle's front
My Lord will have need of me.
But if, by a still, small voice he calls
To paths that I do not know,
I'll answer, dear Lord, with my hand in thine:
I'll go where you want me to go.

—Hymn 270, Verse 1

CHAPTER TWENTY-NINE

"Someday You'll Serve a Mission in Russia"

by Daniel Bay Gibbons

A few days after arriving in Germany in 1976, Elder Kerry Jon Williams, my first companion, and I met a striking-looking man on the street in Duisburg, Germany. He was of average height and build, but had a full black beard and piercing grey eyes. We immediately learned that he was a political refugee from the former Soviet Union, newly arrived in West Germany with his family. He spoke very little German, but invited us to come visit him that evening.

In his tiny apartment, we met his wife and young daughters. The home was plain but very clean and filled with Russian objects, including a samovar on the table and a table covered with candles and icons in the corner. We taught the family a first discussion, which the Russian man translated from German into Russian for his wife. They seemed to hear the message with great interest, but ultimately decided not to hear more.

That evening when we returned to our apartment and prepared to go to sleep, I felt a great peace descend upon me. I thought again and again of this Russian man and his beautiful family, of the photographs and simple artwork from Russia hanging on the walls of their apartment, and of the sense of kinship I felt looking into their faces and their eyes. I then picked up my missionary journal and wrote, "Today we taught a Russian family. The Spirit seems to be whispering to me, 'Someday you'll serve a mission in Russia!' Therefore, I feel like I should study Russian after my mission."

Throughout the rest of my mission, I met many other refugees from Russia and Ukraine and continued to have the impression that I would someday serve a mission in Russia. I also bought a Russian Bible while in Germany, and had a Russian investigator teach me how to say, "I know that God lives" in Russian.

In accordance with these impressions, my first act upon returning to the United States in 1978 was to register for first-year Russian, and through the years I studied the language off and on, as will be discussed later.

In 2011 I was called to serve as a mission president in Russia, thirty-five years after receiving the impression in Germany as a nineteen-year-old missionary. This is a powerful testimony that God does live and that He directs our paths, even over many decades, if we are heedful of the spiritual impressions that come from time to time.

CHAPTER THIRTY

"Immersion in the Spiritual Element"
by Francis M. Gibbons

I arrived in Atlanta, Georgia, in the Southern States Mission in January of 1942. My first assignment was to labor in Lake City, Florida, with Elder Raymond Neeley. We had worked together for several weeks when I was transferred to Jacksonville, Florida, to work with Elder Marion Baird. After a while, Elder Baird and I were transferred to labor in Chiefland, Florida, a rural village in western Florida, from where we walked in all directions, working with people living on isolated farms or in other small villages in close proximity to Chiefland. The work was slow, tedious, relatively unproductive, and quite unsatisfying. Near this time, Elder Wilford Hunter was transferred into our district from South Carolina. Elder Hunter enjoyed the reputation of being one of the hardest-working and most productive missionaries in the Southern States Mission. He consistently stood at or near the top in most categories of proselyting work, hours spent tracting, cottage and street meetings, and baptisms. When he arrived in our district, I had a great desire to work with him. I wanted to see how he did his work and the methods and motivations he used. Toward this end, I began to pray fervently in my secret prayers that if it were the Lord's will that I be permitted to labor with Elder Hunter. In time the Spirit whispered to me that my prayers would be answered, and I duly recorded this prompting in my journal.

In early July 1942, the missionaries in northern Florida were called to Jacksonville for a district conference. I went there with the confident expectation that pursuant to my prayers and the prompting I had received, I would be assigned to labor with Elder Hunter. The conference lasted two days, filled with meetings, instructions, interviews, and social events. Throughout, nothing was said about the thing uppermost in my mind: transfers. I became edgy about it and shortly before the final meeting on the last day, I went to the district president, Mont K. Jensen, and said: "President Jensen, if the conditions ever seem appropriate, I would appreciate the opportunity of working with Elder Hunter." His response was wholly unexpected and very embarrassing. "Elder Gibbons," he said, "we don't ask for positions in the Church," and turning around, walked away. The thought came to me at the time that any hope of receiving the blessing I fervently sought, and assumed I would receive, was gone because of my improper question. But, following the meeting, President Jensen read a list of assignment changes, one of which was that Elder Gibbons was to be transferred from Chiefland to High Springs to labor with Elder Hunter.

Afterward President Jensen came to me and said, "Elder Gibbons. I want you to understand that I assigned you to labor with Elder Hunter, not because of what you said but in spite of what you said. That decision was made several days ago; and when you spoke to me just before the meeting, I almost changed my mind." I should have been content to remain silent and wait patiently for the promise to be fulfilled. The lesson I learned from this experience has served me well over the years. Not once since then have I sought position in the Church, nor have I been impatient about receiving a fulfillment of the blessings promised to me through the Spirit.

I took the bus early one morning from Chiefland to High Springs a few days after the district conference. Soon after I arrived in High Springs, Elder Hunter and I went to work. That afternoon, we arranged for a baptism, had success in tracting, placed a copy of *The Book of Mormon*, and had positive gospel conversations. It was the most productive day of my mission.

That evening as we were washing the dishes from our evening meal in Sister West's kitchen where we boarded, I told Elder Hunter the circumstances under which I had been assigned to labor with him. When I had finished, he looked at me intently and, without preamble, said, "Elder Gibbons, in the name of Jesus Christ I prophesy that if you will remain faithful," and he then uttered a prophecy concerning me. The content of the prophecy was not as significant as was the physical impact it had on both of us and the spiritual knowledge borne upon my soul afterward, which was unrelated to the prophecy. As to the physical impact, Elder Hunter's face seemed to pale as he uttered the words and it had a different expression and appearance than it normally had. As for me, my breath involuntarily began to come in short gasps, a condition which continued for some time after he had finished speaking. But the most extraordinary thing about the incident was that even while Elder Hunter was speaking, and afterward while the physical conditions I have mentioned continued, there came into my mind and whole being the sure knowledge that God lives, that Jesus Christ is His Son and that The Church of Jesus Christ of Latter-day Saints is true. I have assumed that the experience was akin to the immersion in the spiritual element described by Lorenzo Snow when he received his witness of the Spirit following his baptism near Kirtland, Ohio, in June of 1836. From that day, July 7, 1942, to this I have been able to testify honestly of my own knowledge that these things are true. The knowledge did not come from the words of any man, but came from the sure witness of the Holy Ghost to my soul. Neither the words, nor the conduct or misconduct of any person can have any impact on that testimony and witness, for it came from God directly to me by spiritual means. I cannot explain how or why it came. I only know it did come, and that since then I have been able to bear an honest and a true witness of these things. And I now bear that witness to my descendants for whom this account is being written. I know God lives; I know that Jesus Christ His Only Begotten Son lives; and I know that this same Jesus is the head of the Church, which bears His name and of which I am a member; I know that Joseph Smith was and is a prophet of the living God, that he was raised up to usher in the dispensation of the fullness of times and that all of those who have followed him in the prophetic line, up to and including the incumbent prophet were and are prophets of the living God; and I bear this witness of my own knowledge and in the name of Jesus Christ, Amen.

This experience that I had as a young man twenty-one years old has profoundly influenced and, in a sense, has dominated my life during all the intervening years. Practically everything I have done since then of any long-term importance or significance has been done in reference to the prophecy and the resulting witness I received on July 7, 1942.

CHAPTER THIRTY-ONE

Seven Spiritual Experiences
by Daniel Bay Gibbons

During my growing-up years I had many simple but personally significant spiritual experiences, which affected my life dramatically. These experiences not only helped me to prepare to go forth as a missionary at age nineteen, but really laid a firm spiritual foundation for the rest of my life. Here are seven experiences, which were a blessing to me during my preparation for missionary service:

First, during my childhood one of my best friends was stricken with leukemia. He missed an entire year of school, his weight dropped to only fifty pounds or so, and for a time he lay very close to death. One day my mother came to me and told me that my friend was not expected to live. Later that day, while in my room, I went in my clothes closet, where no one would see me, and knelt down and prayed for my friend's life. At the time I had a powerful sense of peace and comfort for my own well-being and that of my friend. His cancer eventually went into complete remission, and he lived to fill a mission, marry, have a family, and pursue his normal adult activities of work and service.

Second, one night as a boy I prayed by my bedside for forgiveness of my sins and transgressions. I must have been eight or ten years old; at this distance it's hard to imagine how serious those sins could have been, but in my mind it was a serious matter. Following my prayer I fell immediately asleep, and upon waking up the next morning I had the most powerful feeling of cleanliness and wholeness and peace.

Third, soon thereafter, I had an experience while reading the New Testament one night in my father's large downstairs library. At the time I was struggling with severe problems with my eyes, including extremely poor vision in my right eye, and weak eye muscles, which prevented my eyes from working together. My eye condition made it hard for me to play sports, as I could not focus clearly upon the ball or have an accurate perception of depth. Also, because my eyes did not always work together, I was often teased, and I was very concerned about what the future might hold for me. As I read the account of Jesus healing the two blind men from the ninth chapter of Matthew, I suddenly felt an impulse to pray for the healing of my eyes. I knelt down beside my father's reading chair, and prayed sincerely for my eyes to be healed. After a long while I opened my eyes, and though I did not see clearly and straightly, I felt a powerful sense of peace and warmth and rightness. As I ponder this more than four decades after the fact, I can see clearly and with perfect straightness due to corrective lenses and muscle surgery performed on my eyes in 1995, and I now know that the Lord has healed me in his own way and time. I also recognize these childhood experiences were my earliest personal glimpses of the power of the atonement of Jesus Christ and the comfort and guidance of the Spirit.

Fourth, for some reason I acquired a youthful fascination with and desire to learn the Russian language. This arose when I discovered a Russian language book in Dad's library. The book was written by Professor Andrey Anastasian of the University of Utah, who later translated *The Book of Mormon* into Russian. I remember poring over this blue-covered book and the strange characters in the Cyrillic alphabet by the hour in the "club house" I occupied in the loft of our garage. This childhood attraction to things Russian later grew as I studied basic Russian in one of my elementary school grades, and then more formal Russian under Valois Zarr at East High School, and ultimately at the University of Utah following my mission. In this I see the hand of the Lord, preparing me for my future service as a missionary in Russia.

Fifth, I vividly remember walking downstairs to our home library one morning and seeing my father inside on his knees praying. I quietly retreated back upstairs, but pondered this event deeply, as it taught me that my father's private religious devotion was in harmony with his public teaching as a bishop and stake president.

Sixth, I remember walking by my mother's little second story study one evening and seeing her sitting at her desk reading with tears streaming down her cheeks. When I asked her what was the matter, she told me that she had been rereading *The Book of Mormon* and that it had just been manifested to her, again, by the Spirit that the book was true.

Seventh, in about 1972, a young single woman and convert to the Church named Annie Osborn was called as my Sunday School teacher. Annie was a medical doctor and professor at the University of Utah, and she became the most influential teacher of my life. One of the first lessons she taught our class was on the power of fervent and prolonged prayer. Shortly after this lesson, I lay awake late one night pondering the things she had said, and I knelt down and really poured out my heart to God, praying with real intent for a period of a couple of hours. As I prayed I felt an all-encompassing peace and warmth, which remained with me throughout my prayer and lingered for many days thereafter. From this time, I began a habit of engaging in fervent and prolonged and highly-directed prayer. Shortly after these events, I one day was hiking over the sagebrush foothills between Fort Douglas and This is the Place Monument and came upon an old military cemetery with green grass beneath very old trees. At the time this cemetery was in the middle of nowhere at the end of a dirt road; the area around it has since been fully developed into the University Research Park. Finding myself alone in this beautiful setting I knelt down and prayed. Over the next several years, and, in fact, well into my adulthood, I have retired to this place many, many times for prayer and pondering; and it is here, in my own Sacred Grove, as it were, that I have made the most significant decisions of my life.

CHAPTER THIRTY-TWO

My Last Visit with Nana

by Daniel Bay Gibbons

My grandmother, Adeline Christensen Gibbons, lived with our family from the time I was about four years old until her death a few months before my mission. We called her "Nana," and she became one of the closest friends and influences of my life. She was one of the first children of European heritage born in the Little Colorado River basin of Arizona, and as a boy I loved to hear her relate stories of frontier Arizona and life in a small Mormon community in the great empty spaces of the West. She had been a widow for many years when she moved to Salt Lake City to be with us, and she died in her nineties.

As my father, Francis M. Gibbons, has described, Nana had a remarkable spiritual experience in 1940 or early 1941, shortly after the death of her husband, my grandfather, Judge Andrew Smith Gibbons. She related that one Sunday morning Grandpa appeared to her and said, referring to my father, "Go get the boy up and get him to priesthood meeting!" That was the entire message, but its effect was to transform the spiritual life of an entire family for generations.

Shortly before Nana's death I had a very memorable spiritual experience while sitting and visiting with her at her bedside one afternoon. This experience affected me greatly and strengthened my testimony in the reality of the spiritual realm and of our immortality beyond the grave. During our conversation, Nana suddenly closed her eyes and appeared to drift off to sleep. After a short time she began to talk, quietly and as if to herself, and seemed to describe things she was then seeing. She described with great alarm her approach to some precipice or barrier, which she obviously feared greatly. She described in a crescendo of emotion that, "It's getting nearer, it's getting nearer, here it comes, I'm going to fall, I'm going to fall."

Then Nana caught her breath, as it were, and uttered the most deep and joyful and heartfelt sigh and expression that I ever heard passes her lips, and said, "Oh! There you are! Come here!" At that moment, I had the powerful impression that she was seeing a vision of my grandfather, Judge Andrew Smith Gibbons, and while I did not see him present, I most surely felt his presence in the room. I also had the impression at that time that the veil is indeed thin, and that our departed loved ones have continuing claim upon us and interest in our life's course. Nana then fell into a deep sleep, and after many minutes I quietly left her bedside and room. This was the last time I had a conversation with Nana before her death.

A few days later, on October 26, 1975, she died peacefully in her bed, in her ninety-second year.

CHAPTER THIRTY-THREE

A Dream of the Road to Rome

by Daniel Bay Gibbons

n the fall of 1876 a Mormon missionary was walking alone along a dusty road on his way to Rome, Georgia, when he came upon a tree standing in a fork in the road. The missionary was John Morgan, and this was, perhaps, the defining moment of his life. Something about this tree in the road stirred up the memory of a dream he had had one night, ten years before.

John Morgan's path to the gospel had taken a wide and circuitous route. Born in Indiana in 1842, at the age of twenty, John enlisted in the Union Army and served in the Civil War with distinction as an officer of the 123rd Regiment of Mounted Infantry. After the war, he enrolled in Eastman's Commercial College in Poughkeepsie, New York, where he graduated in 1866. After graduation he signed a contract to drive a herd of cattle from Kansas City, Missouri, to Salt Lake City.

Salt Lake City appealed greatly to John, though he was not a member of the Church. He soon found a place to live in the home of Joseph L. Heywood, who was then the bishop of the 17th Ward. Deciding to settle permanently in Utah, John became a teacher and founded a college, which he named the Morgan Commercial College. Eventually this college boasted an enrollment of seven hundred students, and was for a time the largest educational institution in Utah Territory.

One night while living in Bishop Heywood's home, John had a vivid dream, which left a great impression on him. In the dream, John saw Brigham Young standing by a tree in a fork in the road. President Young told John that the right hand fork would lead him to Rome, but that if he would take the left-hand fork, it would lead him to a sacred experience which would prove to him the divinity of *The Book of Mormon* and the gospel as taught by The Church of Jesus Christ of Latter-day Saints. The dream troubled John, because at the time he had not even considered joining the Church. However, he did relate the dream to his landlady, Sister Sarepta Blodgett Heywood, and asked her what she thought of it. Sister Heywood responded:

> I can give you the interpretation! Some day you will join our Church. You will be sent on a mission for our Church. You will be going over the same road you saw in your dream and will come to that identical fork in the road. You will recognize that tree. Brigham Young will not be there, but don't forget what he told you. Act upon his counsel.

John did indeed join the Church, as prophesied by Sister Heywood, and was, within a few years, called on a mission; and now he stood at the identical fork in the road as he had seen in his dream. Just as in his dream, the right-hand fork led to Rome—that is Rome, Georgia, his intended destination. Recalling Sister Heywood's advice to follow Brigham Young's counsel, John took the left-hand fork, which soon led him to a place that, surprisingly, was called Haywood Valley.

The Spirit burned within John as the road led him through the beautiful valley, bright with autumn colors. He found that there were about twenty-five to thirty farms in the valley. He stopped at the first home, and was invited to stay for supper. After the meal, the family gathered together—father, mother and children—and he taught them about the Church, and how the Bible had testified of the coming of *The Book of Mormon* and the restoration of the gospel in the latter-days. The Spirit was present in abundance, and the entire family was greatly excited about his message. John was invited to stay the night, but before retiring, the father of the family pulled out his family Bible and opened it to the very scriptures that John had referred to in his teaching. Every single passage quoted by John was underlined in red in the old family Bible. The father went on to explain that about ten days earlier a stranger had visited the family and spent some time with them. He had marked the passages in the family Bible, and had explained that within a few days another man would visit them and expound on the meaning of these marked scriptures and share with them the purpose of this life.

Over the next several days, John found to his great amazement that every family in the Haywood Valley, with a few exceptions, had been visited by the same stranger, who had marked their Bibles and told them that another man would soon come to give them the fullness of the gospel. Within a few weeks John baptized all of these families into the Church, including a Methodist minister, who turned over his Church to Elder Morgan. A branch of the Church was formed, and John Morgan became the presiding elder of the Haywood Branch.

Thus John's dream was fulfilled in a most miraculous manner. Brigham Young's statement in the dream that taking the left-hand fork in the road would provide him with additional evidence of the divinity of *The Book of Mormon* and the Church was literally fulfilled. Upon reflection, John concluded that the mysterious stranger who had thus paved the way for his missionary work in the Haywood Valley might have been one of the Three Nephites, who were promised that they should never taste of death, but should "live to behold all the doings of the Father, unto the children of men, even until all things shall be fulfilled."

John later served as president of the Southern States Mission, and finally as one of the Seven Presidents of the First Council of the Seventy. He died unexpectedly at the age of 52.

CHAPTER THIRTY-FOUR

My Delayed Mission Call
by Daniel Bay Gibbons

In the early spring of 1976, I received my mission call to serve in the Germany Duesseldorf Mission. My call indicated that I was to report to the Language Training Mission on August 19, 1976, even though I was available to report as early as the first week of July. When I entered the LTM, I learned that each of the approximately fifteen elders in my group bound for Duesseldorf had received their calls in about June, while those who had received their calls in the early spring, with mine, had already reported to the LTM in June or July. I thought this was strange, but trusted that there was some reason for the delay in my reporting date.

Soon after arriving in Germany, I had a strong impression that I would ultimately be called to serve as an assistant to my mission president, Hans-Juergen Saager, and I recorded this impression several times in my missionary diary. After serving as the mission secretary for seven months, I was called as an assistant to President Saager in February of 1978 and served in that capacity until my release in early September 1978. On July 1, 1978, President Saager concluded his mission, and he was replaced by President Robert H. M. Killpack, to whom I served as an assistant for some two months.

During the months I served with President Killpack, I was able to witness firsthand the transition of a new mission president. I was also at President

Killpack's side while he dealt with a number of crises in the mission, including the hospitalization of several missionaries and the death of a young German missionary, Elder Dieter Fricke.

Recently, following my service as a mission president in the Russia Novosibirsk Mission, I was pondering again, as I had many times, the strange circumstances of my delayed mission call. At the distance of more than thirty-five years, it is now evident to me that my call to Germany was delayed by the Lord for the specific purpose of allowing me to witness the transition of a full-time mission president.

CHAPTER THIRTY-FIVE

Vision of a Special Book
by Daniel Bay Gibbons

Alexander Neibaur, poet, scholar, and linguist, was the first Jewish convert to The Church of Jesus Christ of Latter day Saints. A remarkable sequence of events, including a "night vision" of a "special book," prompted Alexander to abandon his rabbinical training and leave his wealthy family. Spiritual impressions then brought him to England, where he was placed in the path of the Church's first foreign missionaries.

Alexander Neibaur was born on January 8, 1808, into a wealthy Jewish family in the German fortress city of Ehrenbreitstein on the Rhine River (now part of Koblenz, Germany). His father, Nathan Neibaur, was a brilliant scholar who had served Napoleon as a linguist and interpreter before becoming a medical doctor. Young Alexander's family intended that he become a rabbi, and so from an early age he commenced to receive a rigorous orthodox religious training. Eventually Alexander mastered seven languages: German, French, English, Hebrew, Greek, Latin and Spanish. Sensitive also to the language of the Spirit, at age seventeen Alexander heeded a spiritual prompting to abandon his rabbinical training and, to the sorrow of his family, left home and entered the University of Berlin to study dentistry. After his graduation in 1828, he traveled extensively throughout Europe. During this time he was converted to Christianity, an event that likely placed a further strain on his relations with his wealthy family, for soon thereafter he left his family and moved to England where he established a dental practice in the city of Preston. In 1834 he married Ellen Breakel, and the couple settled down in a home near Preston's famous "Cock Pit," which was one of the largest meeting places of the period outside of London.

Alexander's deep spirituality, coupled with the proximity of the Neibaur's home and dental office to the Cock Pit, was to have vast and unforeseen impact on the future course of their lives. Alexander frequently experienced "night visions," as he called them, or prophetic dreams. In 1837 he had a vivid and powerful dream in which he beheld a special book, which he understood he was to seek out. Soon thereafter, the first Mormon missionaries arrived in England and soon came to preach in Preston because of the large potential audience that could be seated in the Cock Pit.

The arrival of the missionaries caused a great stir in the neighborhood. One morning as Ellen Neibaur was whitewashing the front steps of their home, a neighbor asked if Ellen had seen the strange missionaries from America who claimed to have a book revealed by an angel. Alexander, who had overheard this exchange through the open window, leaned out with great excitement and asked the neighbor where he might find these men from America. Learning their address, he went immediately to the lodging place of the missionaries and there met Heber C. Kimball and Orson Hyde, both members of the Quorum of the Twelve, as well as Elder Willard Richards, a future member of the Twelve. His first question to these brethren was, "You have a book?" Obtaining a copy of *The Book of Mormon*, he recognized it as the book he had seen in his "night visions." Alexander read *The Book of Mormon* over the next three days and returned to request baptism. The missionaries, perhaps knowing of his Jewish heritage and wanting irrefutable evidence of Alexander's conversion, asked him to wait until spring. After waiting the required period, Alexander presented himself to the Apostles and declared, "Gentlemen, I am prepared!" He was baptized in the River Ribble on April 9, 1838.

Ellen Neibaur's conversion to the gospel is no less remarkable than that of her husband. Though she did not oppose Alexander's baptism, she was initially quite cool toward the missionaries and dismissed *The Book of Mormon* as a "pretty story" fabricated by imposters. However, soon thereafter she, too, had a remarkable dream in which she saw Willard Richards' face outlined in the clouds of the sky. Interpreting this to mean that the heavens approved of the missionaries' message, Ellen also accepted baptism.

In 1841 Alexander and Ellen and their young children sold everything they owned and joined an emigrant company of English saints bound for Nauvoo, where they arrived in April of 1841. In Nauvoo, Alexander reestablished his dental practice, initially in Brigham Young's living room, and supplemented his income by working as a day laborer on the temple and the Nauvoo House, as a translator and as a language tutor.

Within days after arriving in Nauvoo, Alexander met the Prophet Joseph Smith for the first time. The Prophet soon engaged Alexander to instruct him in both German and Hebrew, and this began a great friendship between the two men. Alexander later replaced teeth of the Prophet, which had been knocked out on one occasion when the Prophet had been tarred and feathered by a mob. Alexander, who kept a faithful diary in Nauvoo, later wrote the following account of the First Vision as given to him by the Prophet:

> "Called at Brother J. S [Joseph Smith's]…Br Joseph told us the first call he had a Revival meeting his mother & Br & Sist got Religion, he wanted to get Religion too wanted to feel & shout like the Rest but could feel nothing, opened his Bible [to] the first Passage that struck him was if any man lack wisdom let him ask of God who giveth to all men liberallity & upbraidat not went into the Wood to pray kneelt himself down his tongue was closet cleavet to his roof—could utter not a word, felt easier after a while = saw a fire towards heaven came near & nearer saw a personage in the fire light complexion blue eyes a piece of white cloth drawn over his shoulders his right arm bear after a wile a other person came to the side of the first Mr Smith then asked must I join the Methodist Church = No = they are not

my People, [all] have gone astray there is none that doeth good no not one, but this is my Beloved son harken ye him, (Journal of Alexander Neibaur, May, 24, 1844.)

In addition to his dental practice and manual labor in Nauvoo, Alexander continued his scholarly pursuits. A gifted writer, he wrote and published many poetic works, including the hymn "Come, Thou Glorious Day of Promise," which is still sung in the Church today. His biblical scholarship was also profound. In 1843 he published in *The Times and Seasons* a detailed discussion regarding Judaic views on the resurrection, citing nearly a dozen works available only in Hebrew. After the death of Joseph and Hyrum Smith in 1844, Alexander wrote and published a long elegiac poem, with a remarkable Hebrew feeling, entitled "Lamentation - Of a Jew Among the Afflicted and Mourning Sons and Daughters of Zion, at the Assassination of the Two Chieftains in Israel, Joseph and Hyrum Smith."

In 1846, the Neibaur's left Nauvoo and made their way to Salt Lake City, where Alexander again established his dental practice. He lived a long and fruitful life, surrounded by his family. His descendants include President Charles W. Nibley, member of the First Presidency, and Hugh Nibley, scholar and writer. Alexander Neibaur died in Salt Lake City on December 15, 1883. His last words were the names of Joseph and Hyrum Smith.

CHAPTER THIRTY-SIX

The Professor's Dream
by Daniel Bay Gibbons

n 1878, Dr. Plotino C. Rhodakanaty, a professor of Greek at a well-known Mexico City College, was about to begin his daily lecture when a small boy entered the classroom and offered to sell a book to the professor. The professor at first refused and tried to dismiss the boy, but then recalled a vivid dream he had received the previous night.

In 1875, a small band of LDS missionaries, led by Daniel Webster Jones, was sent for the first time to the nation of Mexico. These elders labored in northern Mexico for some months without baptizing a single person. Their mission was far from a failure, however. Before returning to Salt Lake City, they planted an important seed by arranging for the publication of a small booklet in Spanish. This little book was entitled *Trozos Selectos del Libro de Mormon* (Choice Selections from the Book of Mormon). Copies of this book were mailed to many well-known citizens and government officials in Mexico in 1875 before the elders returned to the United States.

Some three years later, this gospel seed bore fruit, as one of the little books fell miraculously into the hands of Dr. Plotino C. Rhodakanaty, a professor of Greek living and teaching in Mexico City. Dr. Rhodakanaty was the son of a Greek father and a Mexican mother. He was a highly learned man, who knew several languages and was a professor of the Greek language at Mexico City's Presbyterian College. At the 1880 General Conference of the Church, Elder Moses Thatcher of the Council of the Twelve described the circumstances under which this little book, *Trozos Selectos del Libro de Mormon*, came into Dr. Rhodakanaty's hands:

> There is a Dr. Rhodacanaty, who is, I believe, a Greek on the side of his father and a Mexican on the side of his mother. He had been engaged in a socialistic work, having for its object the benefitting of the poorer classes— seeking to organize a system, in some respects like our co-operative system here, for the intelligent direction of labor, and, having used his influence in this direction for a short time, he became perplexed, and his mind seemed to close down, so that he could not see how to make further progress. He therefore felt to pray to the Lord to give him wisdom to proceed. During the night he dreamed that a person came and presented to him a book, pressing it emphatically upon his forehead. On the following day, while teaching his class in the college, wherein he was Greek Professor, a little boy entered and asked him to buy a book. "No," said he to the boy, "I do not want your book." "But," says the boy, "you do want this book, and it is only a riel" (twelve and a half cents). He told the boy again that he did not want the book, but the boy still insisted that he did, and finally he took it. When he came to read the book, it proved to be that part of the Book of Mormon which has been translated into the Spanish language. (Moses Thatcher, Conference Report, April 1880, p. 18.)

Dr. Rhodakanaty commenced to read the book, which contained a part of *The Book of Mormon* in Spanish. Having many questions about the doctrine contained in the book, Dr. Rhodokanaty wrote several letters to President John Taylor, President of the Church, inquiring about the principles of the gospel. Several Church publications were forwarded to Dr. Rhodokanaty by the Office of the First Presidency in the fall of 1878, and Dr. Rhodokanaty studied these diligently with many of his friends. Eventually about fifteen or twenty citizens of Mexico City came to believe the truth of the gospel and organized themselves into an informal group, led by Dr. Rhodokanaty.

The similarities between the conversions of Dr. Rhodokanaty and his friends in Mexico City in the 1870's and those of William Billy Johnson, Anthony Obinna, and others in West Africa in the 1970's is striking. In both cases *The Book of Mormon* fell into the hands of a spiritually minded and influential man who converted many to the truth on his own and wrote letters to the President of the Church pleading for missionaries. And in both cases, the first missionaries sent by the prophet experienced immediate success in baptizing many converts to the Church.

In the case of Dr. Rhodokanaty, President John Taylor called Elder Moses Thatcher to go to Mexico City to meet the professor and open the missionary work to the nation of Mexico. In company with two companions, Elder Thatcher arrived in Mexico City on the evening of Saturday, November 16, 1878. The following afternoon Dr. Rhodakanaty visited the Apostle. Elder Thatcher found him to be "a cultured and well educated gentleman," and was surprised to learn that during the preceding months Dr. Rhodakanaty had been publishing a monthly periodical called *Voz del Desierto*, which advocated the principles of the gospel. Elder Thatcher immediately baptized Platino C. Rhodakanaty and Silviano Artiago. Six other men were baptized into the Church two days later. At the meeting where these eight new converts were confirmed, Elder Thatcher organized the first branch of the Church in Mexico, and set apart Dr. Rhodokanaty to preside over it. By the end of 1878, sixteen persons had been baptized, thus laying the foundation for a great missionary work in the nation of Mexico.

The Lord has said, "Out of small things proceedeth that which is great." (D&C 64:33). That truth of that statement is certainly proved true in the experience of Dr. Rhodakanaty's dream of a special book.

CHAPTER THIRTY-SEVEN

Prophets, Seers and Revelators

by Daniel Bay Gibbons

Though I had grown up with the blessing of personal acquaintance with many of the General Authorities, my real spiritual testimony of the calling of the First Presidency and the Twelve as Prophets, Seers, and Revelators was first obtained by me in the mission field. As a boy I had personally met three Presidents of the Church, President Joseph Fielding Smith, President Harold B. Lee, and President Spencer W. Kimball, through my father, who served as secretary to the First Presidency. In addition, I was acquainted with many other Apostles who lived in the Bonneville Stake, including President Hugh B. Brown, President Marion G. Romney, Elder Mark E. Peterson, and Elder Richard L. Evans. Brethren who I personally knew who later became members of the Quorum of the Twelve included Elder Russell M. Nelson, Elder Joseph B. Wirthlin, and Elder Neal A. Maxwell. The Language Training Mission was dedicated during my time there on September 27, 1986. Among those in attendance were President Kimball, President Romney, Elder LeGrand Richards, President Ezra Taft Benson, Elder Thomas S. Monson, Elder Bruce R. McConkie, Elder Boyd K. Packer, Elder L. Tom Perry, Elder David B. Haight, and Elder James E. Faust. As I sat among the 1,300 missionaries who attended the dedicatory service and saw the members of the Twelve and the other General Authorities file in to sit on the stand, I had a profound manifestation of the Spirit that these were truly special witnesses of the Lord. And then as President Kimball and his party arrived a few minutes before 9:00 a.m., and I stood with all of the assembly, I felt an overwhelming manifestation of the Spirit, almost as if a great wind filled the room, which brought tears to my eyes, and I had born in me a testimony that here was the mouthpiece of the Lord. From that day to this I have been able to bear testimony that these are truly Prophets, Seers, and Revelators.

CHAPTER THIRTY-EIGHT

Three Dreams of a Beautiful Building

by Daniel Bay Gibbons

Three remarkable dreams of "a most beautiful building" intrigued and inspired Anthony Uzodimma Obinna. In 1971 he found a picture of the building of his dream reproduced in a magazine — it was the Salt Lake Temple. Anthony's spiritual journey led ultimately to the conversion of his entire family and helped open the door to the preaching of the gospel in his native Nigeria. He was the first convert baptized in West Africa in this dispensation.

Born in 1928 in Umuelem Enyiogugu, Nigeria, Anthony Uzodimma Obinna was named "Uzodimma," which means "the best way," and "Obinna," which means "one who is very dear to his father." Anthony grew up in a large and loving family. Though his parents and grandparents were, in Anthony's words, "idol worshippers," they were good people who led peaceful lives according to the light that God had given them. Anthony recalls that his father "was an influential man, a peacemaker, a lover of truth, a local judge, and one who opposed evils and lies." Anthony was sent to school by his parents in 1937, though that was a rare occurrence for young people from his village. Eventually Anthony became a schoolteacher. At the encouragement of a Catholic priest Anthony had befriended, he took correspondence courses in English, geography, history and religion from Wolsey Hall in Oxford, England. In 1950 he married Fidelia Njoku, who had converted to Catholicism. Before their marriage, Fidelia told Anthony that "God was directing all her affairs because of the very strong faith she had in Him."

In November of 1965 Anthony had a vivid dream in which he was visited by "a tall person carrying a walking stick in his right hand." This dream recurred in 1969 and again in 1970. In the dream, the tall personage took Anthony "to a most beautiful building and showed me everything in it." This dream had a powerful impact on Anthony, and he related it to his wife and his brothers. Several months later he was confined to his house during the Nigerian civil war, and lacking reading material, he picked up a *Reader's Digest* for September 1958. On page 34 of the magazine, he saw a picture of the exact building he had been shown in his three dreams. It was an article about The Church of Jesus Christ of Latter-day Saints and the picture was of the Salt Lake Temple. Anthony recalled: "From the time I finished reading the story, I had no rest of mind any longer. My whole attention was focused on my new discovery. I rushed out to tell my brothers, who were all amazed and astonished to hear the story."

At the conclusion of the civil war in 1971, Anthony was able to send letters to Church headquarters in Salt Lake City, and he opened up a correspondence with the First Presidency and the Church's Missionary Department. In one of the letters he stated:

> We here are the true sons of God, but colour makes no difference in the service of Our Heavenly Father and Christ. The Spirit of God calls us to abide by this Church and there is nothing to keep us out. (*Ensign*, February 1980, page 74).

Copies of *The Book of Mormon* and other literature were sent to the Obinna family. Soon the entire family was converted to the truth of the restored gospel. This was a difficult time for Anthony and his family members. They studied the gospel with great excitement and conviction, but faced much persecution because of their new beliefs. But Anthony recalls: "I knew I had discovered the truth and men's threats could not move me and my group. So we continued asking God to open the door for us." Anthony was also blessed by many dreams in which he foresaw the coming of missionaries of the Church.

Anthony's dreams came to pass in November of 1978 when the Church sent the first missionaries to West Africa. On November 21, 1978, Anthony and eighteen others were baptized into the Church. The Aboh Branch was then organized, with Anthony as branch president, his brothers Francis and Raymond as his counselors, and his wife Fidelia as the Relief Society President. Nearly all of Anthony's family subsequently joined the Church.

Sister Janath R. Cannon, one of the first missionaries to Africa, had previously served as a counselor in the General Relief Society Presidency, and my wife Julie was her personal secretary. Soon after the organization of the Aboh Branch, Sister Janath R. Cannon wrote this account for Julie and her former associates in the General Presidency:

> This group of people has truly been prepared by the Lord. Their leader, Anthony Obinna, is one of those inspired souls who have been in touch with the Church for many years. He first heard of the Church through a *Readers Digest* article, wrote for literature, and now has a bookcase full of tracts and books, including the Standard Works, copies of the *Ensign* and the *Church News*, and *A Marvelous Work and a Wonder*, all of which he has obviously studied and taught to his extended family. They have a neat, two-room meetinghouse where they have been holding regular Sunday meetings. Brother Obinna is the assistant schoolmaster of the village primary school and is highly respected by the local government authorities and village elders, with whom we met when we arrived for the services. He speaks good English, as do his brothers, but the women and young children require translation. Fidelia, his wife, speaks some English. She is a beautiful woman, a mild-mannered, sweet-faced queen. (Letter from Janath R. Cannon to members of the Relief Society General Board, written 22 November 1978.)

In 1989 Anthony was finally able to see the Salt Lake Temple, the building which he had seen in his dreams so many years before. He and Fidelia were subsequently sealed in the Logan Temple. Anthony died at Aboh Mbaise, Nigeria, on August 25, 1995.

Part Five

Perhaps today there are loving words
Which Jesus would have me speak;
There may be now in the paths of sin
Some wand'rer whom I should seek.
O Savior, if thou wilt be my guide,
Tho dark and rugged the way,
My voice shall echo the message sweet:
I'll say what you want me to say.

—Hymn 270, Verse 2

CHAPTER THIRTY-NINE

Searching for the "Book of Ether"

by Daniel Bay Gibbons

Just after the turn of the nineteenth century, a young Englishwoman, Mary Gardner, experienced the tragic death of her young daughter. During her days of deep mourning, Mary turned to the Bible, seeking for comfort and for answers to painful questions, but she failed to find any peace or consolation. Then one afternoon, three weeks after the child's death, Mary had a remarkable dream— a dream that not only gave her a profound sense of peace, but started her on a life-changing search for a book called "The Book of Ether."

In the early 1900's, Mary Gardner was a young woman living with her husband and little daughter in Birkenhead, England, a busy port town on the Irish Sea. Though Mary and her husband had little means, life was very happy. Raised in a believing Christian family, Mary regularly read from the Bible, though she little understood its teachings. She had heard of "Mormons," who were then very unpopular in England and small in numbers, but she knew virtually nothing of the beliefs of "Mormonism."

In 1904 Mary's idyllic life was shattered when her little girl died suddenly. Mary's grief was deep and profound, and she wondered why God would allow her sweet daughter to suffer death at such a tender age. One Sunday afternoon, three weeks after her daughter's death, Mary sat alone in her bedroom weeping. Seeing her Bible, she picked it up and sought for some special consolation by reading. But as she read, Mary became ever more discouraged and distraught, for the scriptures she read seemed to her to be contradictory. In her grief and despair she lay down on her bed and soon fell asleep. Mary wrote:

> I closed my eyes and fell asleep, but only for a few moments. I saw my little girl, who had passed away. She came into the room in the same way as she used to come when alive. She held an open book in her hand. Presently she held the book out to me and said, "Read mother," and I read at the top of the page, "The Book of Ether." Then I opened my eyes with a start and there was nothing to be seen. There was no one in the room. (*Millennial Star*, August 19, 1915, volume 77, page 523.)

This dream turned out to be one of the central events of Mary's life. She was startled and puzzled by her dream, but also experienced a profound sense of peace. The appearance of her daughter in the dream was very comforting to Mary. Though she still missed her daughter greatly, she felt certain that her little girl was in the hands of God. Mary was also greatly intrigued by the meaning of the book she had seen in her dream, and the words that she had read at the top of the page, "The Book of Ether." She also could not forget her daughter's simple admonition, "Read, Mother!"

In the months and years following the death of her daughter, Mary could not forget her dream of "The Book of Ether." She found herself pondering the dream again and again. Eventually she began to wonder if there actually may be a "Book of Ether," and so Mary began to visit libraries and bookstores where she inquired after a book called "The Book of Ether." No one she spoke with had ever heard of it.

About three years after her dream, Mary began a friendship with a neighbor woman who had recently moved into the neighborhood. Mary had heard rumors that her new friend was one of the "Mormons." Mary's friend even tried to engage Mary in conversation about "Mormonism" and

Joseph Smith. She lent Mary several books and tracts about the Church, but Mary was not particularly interested. Then one day Mary had a life-changing experience:

> One morning I called upon this sister, and was shown into the kitchen to wait for a few minutes before she came. On the table there was a book. I picked it up, and the pages rolled and opened at the Book of Ether. I was astonished. I looked on the cover and saw the name "Book of Mormon." I jumped up immediately and ran to the door and met the lady and told her about my dream. She did not make any particular comment, but lent me the book to take home and read. (*Millennial Star*, August 19, 1915, volume 77, pages 523 to 524.)

Mary took *The Book of Mormon* home with trembling anticipation, to read "The Book of Ether." By the time she next saw her friend, Mary had a firm testimony of the truth of *The Book of Mormon* and the gospel of Jesus Christ. Soon Mary was baptized and joined herself to the little congregation of "Mormons" in Birkenhead, England, grateful that the Lord had permitted her to heed her little girl's simple admonition: "Read, Mother!"

CHAPTER FORTY

Training Up a Prophet
by Francis M. Gibbons

other of Heber J. Grant, the seventh president of The Church of Jesus Christ of Latter-day Saints, Rachel Ridgway Ivins Grant, was a woman of great spirituality who humbly and carefully prepared her fatherless son for his future role of leadership in the Church.

Rachel Ivins was born March 7, 1821, in Hornerstown, New Jersey. A member of the Baptist Church, Rachel first heard about the Mormon church at a Sunday meeting she chanced to attend where two elders spoke. As she had heard derogatory things about the Mormons and had been warned by her pastor not to attend their meetings, she kneeled that night and asked the Lord to forgive her for doing such a thing on the Sabbath. However, she was intrigued by what the elders had said and by literature she had been given. This induced her to attend other meetings where she became deeply immersed in Mormon doctrine. Aware of what she was doing, her Baptist minister threatened to disfellowship Rachel unless she desisted. Annoyed by this clumsy attempt to intrude on her independence, Rachel ignored the minister and continued to attend the Mormon meetings. When at last she was convinced the message of the missionaries was true, Rachel was baptized and confirmed as a member of The Church of Jesus Christ of

Latter-day Saints. With this came the urge to gather with the Saints in Nauvoo, Illinois.

Here Rachel's understanding of the Church became more complete and compelling as she listened to Joseph Smith and other Church leaders expound Mormon doctrine. She also was pleased with the cultural climate she found in Nauvoo, the women's Relief Society, the dramatic and manual arts, the literary clubs, and the social events. When the Latter-day Saints were expelled from Nauvoo, she joined the exodus, migrating with her sister Anna and brother-in-law, first to Winter Quarters and then to the Salt Lake Valley where they arrived August 10, 1853. Two years later she married Jedediah M. Grant, second counselor in the First Presidency of the Church.

Rachel's only child, Heber Jeddy Grant, was born November 22, 1856. Nine days later, the child's father died. In remarks made at the funeral, President Brigham Young said,

> Brother Grant we call a great man, a giant, a lion; but let me tell you that the young whelps who are growing up here will roar louder than ever he dare, and . . . the very sons of these women that sit here will rise up and be as great as any man that ever lived, and as far beyond Jedediah or myself, and Brother Heber, as we are in the gospel beyond our little children.

Several months later, Rachel received further insight into the role her son would play. At a Relief Society meeting, Eliza R. Snow, in bearing her testimony, pointed at young Heber, who was crawling on the floor, and, speaking in tongues, predicted that the infant would ultimately stand as one of the high leaders of the Church, providing motivation and direction for thousands of Latter-day Saints. The interpretation of the prophecy was made by Zina D. Young, another wife of President Brigham Young. From then until Heber was a grown man, Rachel urged him to guard his thoughts and actions because the Lord had an important work for him to perform. Heber, who had no recollection of either President Young's sermon or the prophecy of Eliza R. Snow, was inclined to discount the mother's admonitions as being the natural feelings of any mother. But when he was called as a stake president at age twenty-four and as a member of the Quorum of the Twelve Apostles at age twenty-six, the mother's counsel was seen in a different light. His call to the Twelve, of course, foreshadowed his ordination as the President of the Church in 1918.

For several years after the death of Jedediah M. Grant, Rachel and Heber shared the Grant home with other wives and children of the deceased. The home was located on the east side of South Main Street. When financial concerns made it necessary to sell the large family home, the wives and their children then moved into separate quarters. Rachel and Heber moved into a small home on Second East Street near First South, which was in the Thirteenth Ward.

Rachel was the Relief Society president of the Thirteenth Ward for thirty-five years. Working with her bishop, Edwin D. Wooley, Rachel faithfully served the needs of members of the ward without compensation, other than the satisfaction of doing her duty.

In her last years, she suffered the burden of deafness, yet rejoiced in the apostolic service of her son, Heber, and in her growing family. She died January 27, 1909, at the home of a granddaughter, Mrs. George J. Cannon.

CHAPTER FORTY-ONE

"I know that The Book of Mormon is true"

by Daniel Bay Gibbons

entered the mission field believing that *The Book of Mormon* was true, but not knowing. Growing up among many active Latter-day Saint youth, I often felt inferior spiritually, as I had never had one landmark experience that I felt would qualify me to say I know that *The Book of Mormon* is true. I remember that my best friend, from about the age of twelve, would often stand up in fast meeting and bear fervent testimony that he *knew The Book of Mormon* was true. Though I had read *The Book of Mormon* several times, and believed it was true, I never said, I know it's true. Consequently, whenever I bore testimony, even at my missionary farewell in 1976, I never stated, "I know *The Book of Mormon* is true."

As I began my mission, I began praying with all the fervency I could muster for some manifestation that *The Book of Mormon* was true. On January 6, 1977, while serving in Duisburg, Germany, I had a powerful experience while reading *The Book of Mormon* aloud with my companion, Elder Kerry Jon Williams. The event recorded in my diary of that date, followed many days of nearly unceasing fervent prayer for a greater witness of the Spirit:

I prayed to the Lord this morning, as last night, that he would show me great things, that he would grant me great spiritual gifts according to my faith and diligence. We began our study class at 7:30. Elder Williams asked me to say a prayer, after which we sang two hymns. I began reading aloud out of the German Book of Mormon in Alma 30, starting with verse 30. By the time I had read three verses, I was so overcome with the Holy Ghost that I couldn't go on, and I was completely overcome. Never has the Spirit moved so strong within me. After many minutes of silence my companion, seeing me in tears, asked me what was the matter. I responded by saying, in German, "Ich weiss dass das Buch Mormon wahr ist." ("I know that *The Book of Mormon* is true.")

I am grateful for this testimony, though it came to me later than many of my friends and companions. This testimony has stood the test of time, and I am thankful to still proclaim, in German, Russian, or English, "I know that *The Book of Mormon* is true!"

CHAPTER FORTY-TWO

"Read the Book"
by Daniel Bay Gibbons

John Wells of Nottingham, England, strongly disapproved of the Mormon church, even though his oldest and best friend had become a member. John went on vacation to the Isle of Man, and one day while alone on the deserted beach he found a copy of The Book of Mormon. *John began to read, but soon threw the book onto the sand. As he did so, however, he heard an audible voice admonishing him to "Read the book!"*

John Wells was born and raised in Nottingham, England. Throughout his boyhood and young adulthood of the 1920's and 1930's, his best and closest friend was a young man named Arthur Winter. For a period of twenty years or more, John and Arthur were almost inseparable companions. They played together in the neighborhood, attended the same schools, went each Sunday to the same parish of the Church of England, and eventually were even hired by the same employer in a large Nottingham company. They also held similar opinions, likes and dislikes. Indeed they were so much alike in personality and upbringing that their respective families jokingly referred to John and Arthur as "twins."

After the two young men had been working at their new jobs for some time, Arthur and his family abruptly moved away to a different city, separating the two for the first time in many years. However, the Winter family soon returned to Nottingham, and Arthur was quickly hired back at his old job, even occupying his old desk next to John's.

During the brief separation of these two friends, a significant event had occurred in the life of Arthur Winter. He and his family had joined The Church of Jesus Christ of Latter-day Saints. In the years before World War II, the Mormons were very unpopular and had a poor reputation in England, particularly among members of the Church of England. Thus, Arthur feared to reveal his conversion to the Mormon church to his friend John and so kept it a secret. When John ultimately discovered that his friend had joined the Mormons, it caused a great rift in their friendship.

Several years after this unfortunate breach in John and Arthur's friendship, John took a long vacation to the Isle of Man. One early morning, John went down to a lonely stretch of beach with his book bag. Leaving his bag on the sand, he took a long walk in the early morning light. When he returned, he thought he would sit down for a while to read. Reaching into his book bag, he was surprised to pull out a copy of *The Book of Mormon*. John was greatly puzzled as to how the book had found its way into his bag, and he looked around on the beach, suspecting that someone had placed it there as a practical joke. Seeing no one, John opened the book and began to read from the first page.

As he read from *The Book of Mormon*, John found himself becoming highly critical of the unusual use of the English language in the book. He had always been a great student of English literature, and after reading a few lines John threw the book onto the sand in disgust. But as he did so, he reported that he heard a distinct and clear voice saying: "Read the Book!"

John again looked around himself to discover who was speaking. No one was in sight. The beach was utterly deserted. Obeying the voice, he picked the book up and again began to read from the first page. Again, John found himself becoming unreasonably critical of the language in the book, and he again dropped it on the sand. A second time he heard a voice saying: "Read the Book!"

John retrieved the book, but instead of reading from the first page as before, he let it fall open at random to one of the last pages, where he read the following:

> And when ye shall receive these things, I would exhort you that ye would ask God, the eternal Father, in the name of Christ, if these things are not true; and if ye shall ask with a sincere heart, with real intent, having faith in Christ, he will manifest it unto you by the power of the Holy Ghost. (Moroni 10:4)

As he read these words, John was particularly struck to the heart by the word "not", in the statement "ask God if these things are *not* true." The word "not" seemed to be a direct challenge to his personal faith in Christ, his sincerity of heart and all that he had ever believed in matters of religion.

During the remaining days of his vacation, John read *The Book of Mormon* from cover to cover, and when he returned to Nottingham, he was soon baptized into the Church.

CHAPTER FORTY-THREE

A Mother's Devotion

by Daniel Bay Gibbons

I t is difficult to imagine having to endure more adversity for the gospel's sake and for the sake of her children than did Mary Fielding Smith. Her greatest quality was her unreserved devotion to the Lord, even in the face of appalling adversity. Born in England into a family of distinction, she saw a great rift develop in that family because of her conversion to the gospel. Married to Patriarch Hyrum Smith, the brother of Joseph, she later endured tragic events surrounding his brutal murder. As a widow, she almost single handedly brought her young children across the American continent to Utah, including the ten-year-old future Church President, Joseph F. Smith.

Mary Fielding Smith was born in Honidon, Bedfordshire, England, the oldest daughter of John and Rachel Fielding. The Fieldings were a close and loving family and devout members of the Wesleyan Methodist Church. In 1834, Mary Fielding left England and immigrated to Toronto, Canada, where she joined her youngest brother, Joseph Fielding, and a younger sister, Mercy Rachel Fielding. In England she left behind many family members, including another brother, James Fielding, who was a prominent Methodist minister. The Canadian Fieldings soon met Elder Parley P. Pratt and accepted the gospel in May of 1836. A great wedge was ultimately to be driven between the American and English branches of the Fielding family because of the conversion of Mary, Joseph, and Mercy. The Reverend James Fielding initially opened his church to Heber C. Kimball and the other missionaries who arrived in England in 1837, but became vehemently opposed to the Church when large numbers of his parishioners began converting. The rift in the family soon became wider and more impassable than the Atlantic Ocean that separated them.

Mary moved to Kirtland in the spring of 1837, and on December 24 of that year she was married to Hyrum Smith, brother of the Prophet Joseph. Hyrum's wife, Jerusha, had recently died leaving him with six motherless children. Mary cared for these orphans as her own. Hyrum and Mary later had two children, Joseph Fielding Smith (who became the sixth president of the Church in 1901) and Martha.

The crucial moment of Mary's life occurred on June 27, 1844, when her beloved husband was brutally murdered in Carthage Jail, leaving her with eight children to care for. Mary, however, had absolute faith that the Lord would always take care of her. Joseph Smith had promised her as much before his death. Mary had once written to a family member that, "The Lord knows what our intentions are, and He will support us and give us grace and strength for the day, if we continue to put our trust in Him and devote ourselves unreservedly to His service." The quality of unreserved devotion to God, even in the face of appalling adversity, is the hallmark of Mary Fielding Smith.

Her qualities of devotion are evident in the events following the martyrdom of her husband. Reduced to almost penniless conditions in Nauvoo, Mary was torn between the desire to maintain the tattered remains of her little family's security and her longing to follow the saints west. Like Emma Smith, she had a difficult decision to make. Mary's was to follow the Twelve Apostles into the wilderness and turn her back forever on the city that had provided so much happiness and tragedy for her and the entire Smith family.

Though she was opposed by others in the Smith family, she gathered up her children and stepchildren and a few possessions and set off with the body of the saints as they streamed westward out of Nauvoo and across the

Mississippi. At Winter Quarters, she was assigned to join the emigrant company of Cornelius P. Lott. Captain Lott told Mary bluntly that she should return back to Winter Quarters and wait for someone to take charge of her and the children. He told her that she would be a burden on the entire emigrant company. She responded in few words that she was proceeding on the journey, and promised that she would beat Captain Lott to the Salt Lake Valley. Thus began a unique race across the Great Plains and the Rocky Mountains to the Salt Lake Valley. Mary had been offended by Captain Lott's gruff manner, and she in turn had surely pricked him by declaring that she would beat him to the Valley.

A few days later as the company was traveling between the Platte and the Sweetwater rivers, one of Mary's oxen lay down in the yoke and appeared to be in the throes of death. All of the wagons following Mary in the company stopped. Soon Captain Lott perceived that half of his wagons had stopped and rode back to investigate. A crowd of pioneers gathered at the scene.

"He is dead," Captain Lott said to men gathered around. "There is no use working with him. We'll have to fix up some way to take the Widow Smith along. I told her she would be a burden to the company."

Mary said nothing, but went to her wagon and returned with a bottle of consecrated oil. She asked her brother, James Fielding, to administer to the fallen ox, believing that the Lord would raise him back up in the yoke. It was a solemn moment and a hush fell over all the saints gathered around her wagon. The men removed their hats, and heads bowed as her brother anointed the fallen ox and prayed over him. The great beast lay stretched out, its eyes glassy. Then, a moment after the administration, the animal stirred. It gathered its legs beneath itself and stood up. Then it started off in the yoke as if nothing had happened.

A short time later, a second ox also lay down on the trail. This time it was Mary's best and strongest ox, "Old Bully." Again, her brother administered to the ox with the same result.

Mary later recollected that James Fielding had been given a blessing by an Apostle, Elder Heber C. Kimball, when they first joined the Church in England. In the blessing Elder Kimball had promised her brother that he would have "power to raise the dead." In the healing of her oxen on the road to Salt Lake City she saw a fulfillment of this special promise.

Mary continued her journey, and her family arrived in the valley a full day ahead of Captain Lott.

The cares of the journey behind her, Mary now had to build a home for her children. She and young Joseph Fielding Smith, assisted by her brother, built a two-room adobe house and cleared land for a garden. In his diary, her brother recorded how the family lost animals, suffered for want of food, and struggled to construct shelters from the cold. After only four years in her new home, she caught a deadly cold and died in 1852 at the age of 51. Her son Joseph F. Smith went on to become an Apostle, a counselor in the First Presidency, and ultimately the sixth President of the Church.

CHAPTER FORTY-FOUR

"You Will Bear a Son"
by Daniel Bay Gibbons

aptized in her native Scotland, Margaret McNeil Ballard learned from an early age the precious nature of the family and the importance of service. At the age of ten, she carried her four-year-old brother on her back as she walked more than a thousand miles from St. Louis, Missouri, to Utah. Her deep love of family was evident throughout her life as she bore and raised a large family of happy children. However, she deeply mourned the deaths of five children who were taken in childbirth or infancy. One day, while praying for consolation she heard a voice promising, "You will bear a son who will become an Apostle of the Lord Jesus Christ." Soon she conceived and bore a son, whom she named Melvin J. Ballard. Like Mary in the New Testament, she kept this precious revelation in her own heart, recording it in her records, but never discussing it with anyone in her family during her lifetime. One year following her death, her son, Melvin J. Ballard, was called to the Quorum of the Twelve Apostles.

In 1854 a small group of Saints walked in the early dawn from their village near Edinburgh, Scotland, to see an eight-year-old girl, Margaret McNeil, be baptized. The waters of the Firth of Forth were icy cold, but the presence of the Spirit filled and warmed her heart. She later wrote: "As I came up out of the water, the day was just beginning to dawn and the light to creep over the eastern hills. It was a very beautiful sight, one that I shall never forget. At this time I was filled with a sweet heavenly spirit which has remained with me to this day." The "sweet heavenly spirit" which Margaret felt came to direct her every action from that day forth. It would lead her from her peaceful homeland halfway across the world to the center stakes of Zion, where she would bear eleven children, serve for thirty years as a president in the Relief Society, and stand at the center of a great family of servants of the Lord. One of her sons, Melvin J. Ballard, became an Apostle, as did her great grandson, M. Russell Ballard.

Within two years of her baptism, Margaret and her family left Scotland for America. While she was sorry to leave her beautiful homeland, she did not miss the great persecution that she had faced since her baptism. She had not been permitted to go to school because she was a Mormon. In St. Louis, Missouri, the McNeils met up with a company of saints who were heading west to the Great Basin. Mother McNeil strapped a four-year-old brother, James, onto Margaret's back and they resolutely set out on the thousand-mile journey to Zion. For nearly the entire journey, Margaret carried little James. This experience strengthened her both physically and spiritually. Later in life she would be called on to bear the burdens of many.

Arriving in Utah, the McNeil family was utterly penniless, yet Margaret soon learned another lesson in her young life—that the Lord provides. On October 4, 1859, the family camped near Ogden, Utah, and Margaret's father went into town to try to find work. "Across the field from where we were was a little home, and out in the yard was a big pile of squash." Margaret wrote. "We were so famished that my mother sent me over to beg for squash, for we did not have a cent of money, and some of the children were very weak for want of food. I knocked at the door, and an old lady came and said, 'Come in, come in. I knew you were coming and have been told to give you food.' She gave me a large loaf of fresh bread and said to tell my mother that she would come over soon. It was not long until she did come and brought us a nicely cooked dinner, something we had not had for a long time. This woman was surely inspired of the Lord to help us, and we were grateful for her kindness. Bread never tasted so good before or since."

The family soon headed further north to Cache Valley, where they settled, and Margaret met and married Henry Ballard. The couple eventually had eleven children, though five died in childbirth or infancy. These deaths were among Margaret's greatest trials. One day, soon after losing two children and having had several miscarriages, Margaret poured out her heart in prayer to the Lord, and was answered with a remarkable revelation. "A voice spoke plainly to her, saying, 'Be of good cheer. Your life is acceptable, and you will bear a son who will become an Apostle of the Lord Jesus Christ.'" Soon after this experience Margaret conceived and bore a son, Melvin Joseph Ballard. Margaret recorded this sacred experience, yet never shared it with anyone during her lifetime. In 1919, a year after her death, Melvin J. Ballard was called to the Quorum of the Twelve Apostles.

Margaret's husband Henry served as a bishop in Logan for thirty-five years. At the same time, Margaret was president of the Relief Society for over thirty years. During this busy period of their lives, Margaret experienced one of the most remarkable spiritual experiences of her life. In 1884, during the week that the Logan Temple was being dedicated, Bishop Ballard was extremely busy writing recommends and attending to the myriad details of the dedicatory services. One day Margaret's young daughter Ellen walked into the Ballard house carrying a newspaper and asked for her father. Margaret told her daughter that the Bishop was busy, and tried to take the newspaper from her hand. Ellen replied, "No, the man who gave me the paper told me to give it to no one but Father." Margaret writes:

> I let the child take the paper to her father, and when he looked it over, he was greatly surprised, for he saw that the paper had been printed in Berkshire, England, his birthplace, and was only four days from the press. He was so amazed at such an incident that he called Ellen and asked her where the man was who had given her the paper. She said that she was playing on the sidewalk with other children when two men came down the street walking in the middle of the road. One of them called to her, saying: "Come here, little girl." She hesitated at first, for there were other little girls with her. Then he pointed to her and said: "You." She went out and

he gave her the paper and told her to give it to her father. The paper contained about sixty names of dead acquaintances of my husband, giving the dates of their birth and death.

Margaret was baptized for the women and Henry for the men in the Logan Temple.

CHAPTER FORTY-FIVE

The Memory of a Mother's Prayers

by Francis M. Gibbons

When David McKay was called to leave his wife and four children to serve a mission for the Church, he hesitated. Only weeks had passed since the deaths of two daughters. Additionally, David's wife, Jennette, had just given birth to a baby. However, David's wife had no hesitation about the mission call. Born in Wales and possessed of a strong will and deep faith in the Lord, Jennette told her husband, "Of course you must accept." David served his mission. During his absence Jennette and their eight-year-old son, future Church President David O. McKay, operated the family farm and finished a major renovation on the house. President McKay often stated that "among my most precious soul treasures is the memory of mother's prayers by the bedside."

Jennette Evans McKay, the mother of David O. McKay, the ninth president of The Church of Jesus Christ of Latter-day Saints, was born August 23, 1850, near Merthyr-Tydfil, South Wales. Jennette's parents, Thomas and Margaret Powell Evans, who were converts to the Church, immigrated to the United States, sailing from Liverpool, England, aboard the packet ship *Horizon* on May 22, 1856. The family arrived in Iowa on July 8,

1856. They remained there three years while Thomas worked to earn enough money to finance their trip across the plains to Utah. They arrived in Salt Lake City on August 18, 1859, with Captain Philip H. Buzzard's company, five days before Jennette's ninth birthday. The Evans family soon travelled to Ogden, Utah, to establish their home.

Fifteen-year-old David McKay saw Jennette seated on the tongue of the family wagon soon after the Evans family arrived in Ogden. David reported later he knew at this moment that Jennette Evans was to be his bride. He never forgot the emotional impact of the young girl's large brown eyes peering at him from beneath a pink sunbonnet. Eight years later, David courted the young Welsh immigrant. Winning Jennette's approval and the approval of her parents, the couple was married in the Salt Lake Endowment House on April 9, 1867, in a ceremony performed by Elder Wilford Woodruff of the Quorum of the Twelve Apostles.

The third child and eldest son of this couple, David Oman McKay, was born on September 8, 1873. The son was always proud of his Welsh ancestry. After his call to the Twelve, Elder David O. McKay attended a stake conference in Malad, Idaho, a community comprised largely of converts from Wales. As he sat on the stand beside the stake president, a pureblood Welshman, Elder McKay whispered that he had Welsh blood in his veins. When the president's manner suggested he thought the visitor's statement was a mere platitude intended to court the favor of the largely Welsh audience, Elder McKay, on standing at the pulpit, reported his comment to the stake president, and the stake president's reaction, then said, "But I wish to say to President Richards and to you that my mother was born in Plasagon House, Cleydyfagwyr Cefn Eved Cwmer, near Merthyr-Tydfil, South Wales, and her name was Evans." At that, an old lady sitting on the front row rose and said, "That's it, that's it, you are, you are."

Jennette not only instilled in David O. and her other children a love for her native land, but, through her actions, she also imbued them with a profound sense of love for family and for the Church. Her love for both was unshaken. "Among my most precious soul treasures" wrote President David O. McKay, "is the memory of mother's prayers by the bedside, of her affectionate touch as she tucked the bedclothes around my brother and me, and gave each a loving goodnight kiss." And her love for the Church was dramatically shown when her husband, David, received a call from the prophet to serve a mission in Great Britain. The timing of the call could not have been more inopportune. Jennette was within weeks of giving birth to her sixth child; it was time for spring planting; and Jennette was still struggling over the loss of her two oldest children, daughters, a few months before. Their deaths left eight-year-old David O. as the oldest living child in the family. These conditions caused David to hesitate in accepting the call. Jennette was adamant. "Of course you must accept," she said. "You need not worry about me. David O. and I will manage things nicely." When David sought counsel from a relative as to whether he should accept, Uncle John Grow answered: "You may be right, and you may be wrong, but if Jennette has set her mind that you should answer the mission call, you might as well give in." David left for the mission field only days before Jennette gave birth to her sixth child. With the help of neighbors, the planting was completed and the harvest was later gathered. Low prices caused Jennette to warehouse her grain until the following year when she sold in a strong market. From the proceeds she went forward with a major renovation of the family home. She and David had discussed this before; but she did not tell him what she was doing. When he returned home from his mission to find the renovation on the home completed, he proudly referred to Jennette as "the greatest miracle that one could ever find."

Jennette McKay's independence and sense of family values surfaced often, but never more noticeably than when she received a substantial legacy from her parent's estate. Family members urged her to invest it to help provide for her old age. She resolutely rejected all such suggestions and instead used the money to help educate her children. The wisdom of her action is seen in the results that followed from it. The contributions these children later made to their church, their communities, and their families were significant, contributions which would have been much less had they lacked the education their mother's generosity helped to provide. Meanwhile, Jennette Evans McKay lived comfortably into old age despite having spent her legacy on the children. She was laid to rest in the picturesque alpine setting of the Upper Ogden Valley, laden with the love, respect, and honor of a grateful progeny.

CHAPTER FORTY-SIX

Three Witnesses

by Daniel Bay Gibbons

President Boyd K. Packer once said in my hearing at a meeting of local priesthood leaders that "The purest form of revelation is the intuition of a righteous woman." The Lord also has repeatedly said that "in the mouths of two or three witnesses" all things are established (*See* Matt. 18:16; 2 Cor. 13:1; D&C 6:28 and D&C 128:3)

The truth of these two statements was demonstrated powerfully in my life in April of 2001, as recorded in this entry from my diary:

I had a remarkable spiritual experience in recent weeks. On Sunday, April 22, 2001, Julie and I took all five of the kids to attend the broadcast dedication of the Winter Quarters Temple at the Cottonwood Stake Center. We arrived more than a half an hour early, as directed, and so we had a long interval for contemplation in the chapel. As we waited, I was praying for help from the Lord regarding my role as a husband and father, my calling as a bishop, my new appointment to a judgeship, my law practice, and our less-than-rosy financial situation in general, and also reading from the Doctrine and Covenants. As I read, I was struck with powerful force over the eleven short verses of Section 111. As I read I had an overpowering impression that there were many lessons in these verses for me. I sat studying the verses for most of the half hour.

Amazingly, later that evening I told Julie about the impressions I had received about Section 111 during the dedication, and she incredulously told me that she had been studying the same verses and having the same impressions during the minutes before the dedication began. This was incredible because Julie and I were sitting at opposite ends of the bench with all of our children between us.

The amazing sequel to this event came several days later when we were with Dad and Mom on the evening of Jenny's solo performance with the Murray Symphony. As I dropped Mom and Dad off at home, I told them the experience Julie and I had received. My Dad then told me that he was dumbfounded while I was telling him of our experience, because only a few days before he had been reading Section 111 and thinking that it held specific messages for Dan. Above all, he said, is the message that I should not worry about money, but that the Lord would provide.

Part Six

"SOME WAND'RER WHOM I SHOULD SEEK"

Perhaps today there are loving words
Which Jesus would have me speak;
There may be now in the paths of sin
Some wand'rer whom I should seek.
O Savior, if thou wilt be my guide,
Tho dark and rugged the way,
My voice shall echo the message sweet:
I'll say what you want me to say.

—Hymn 270, Verse 2

CHAPTER FORTY-SEVEN

The Wanderers' Branch

by Daniel Bay Gibbons

For a few brief years in the 1850's, a mission of the Church flourished in India. Of this effort B. H. Roberts wrote, "there is nothing more heroic in our Church annals than the labors and sufferings of these brethren of the mission to India." One of the most interesting persons converted during this brief mission was an Englishman named Maurice White. Baptized in Calcutta by the first missionary in India, Maurice was ordained to the priesthood and set apart as the presiding local authority in Asia only one week after his baptism. During his brief ministry in India, he was instrumental in bringing the first native Indian people into the Church.

The spreading of the gospel is like the scattering of seeds. Seeds of the gospel are quickly blown and spread and take root in the most unlikely of places. So it is with the humble beginnings of the Church in India in the late 1840's and early 1850's. However, in the case of India, the origin of the first seed was not from Nauvoo, or Salt Lake City, but from England. In the late 1840's, two men, Private Thomas Metcalf of the British army and William A. Sheppard of Calcutta, wrote home to England asking for information about the Church.

At about the same time, the first Latter-day Saints set foot in India. They were George Barber and Benjamin Richey, two British sailors who had been baptized in England on January 27, 1849, who arrived later that year in Calcutta, India. Though Barber and Richey did not hold the priesthood and were not well-grounded in the principles of the gospel, they enthusiastically taught what they knew to other British expatriates in Calcutta, and wrote to Church authorities in England for missionaries to be sent.

As a result of these requests, Elder Joseph Richards was sent to Calcutta in June of 1851. Elder Richards was able to stay in Calcutta only a few days, but he performed the first baptisms in India. These converts were all Englishman, including Maurice White. One week after Maurice White was baptized, Elder Richards ordained Maurice an elder and set him apart as the president of the branch of the Church in Calcutta. This branch was later known as the "Wanderer's Branch." The "Wanderer's Branch" was the first unit of the Church in Asia.

The name "Wanderer's Branch" is very appropriate because all of the members of the branch were, in a sense, wanderers. Most of them were British sailors, soldiers, or businessmen who were far from home and England. They were also very few in number and must have felt rather isolated, not only because they were of a foreign race than the millions of native Indians, but also because they had joined a strange and unpopular religion: Mormonism.

Maurice's service as president of the "Wanderer's Branch" was both very brief and very significant. It was brief because within a few months, he returned to England with the express purpose of learning more about the operation of the Church. Before he left, however, Maurice baptized the first native Indian into the Church—a woman named Anna. On December 25, 1851, another missionary arrived in Calcutta. He was Elder William Willes. Elder Willes had been sent by Lorenzo Snow, who was then president of the Swiss and Italian missions. Elder Willes found only six members of the Church in Calcutta. Elder Richards had returned to London in June; and Maurice White, the first president of the "Wanderer's Branch" had also departed for England to learn more about the Church.

Elder Willes was very gratified to learn of the baptism of Anna by Elder White, and that through her instrumentality an entire congregation of

Episcopalian Christians desired baptism into the Church. Concerning the impending baptisms of these native Indians, Elder Willes wrote:

> Although I am writing in this cool, businesslike strain, my heart is bounding with grateful emotions of thanksgiving that he has made me and my brethren the instruments in His hands for spreading such glorious tidings in a land filled with "darkness, selfishness and cruel habitations." (*Millennial Star* London, England, Vol. XIV, p. 90.)

Nothing is known of the life of Maurice White either before he joined the Church or after he returned to England. However, this "Wanderer" performed an inestimable service to the kingdom in India by bringing the first native Indian converts into the Church.

CHAPTER FORTY-EIGHT

The Miracle Blowout on Ninth South

by Francis M. Gibbons

have had several flat tires in my life, but only one blowout which sounded like a rifle shot. This occurred during my service as a member of the Bonneville Stake High Council in the late 1960's. I was driving east on Ninth South in Salt Lake City near Fifteenth East when it occurred. I immediately pulled to the curb in order to change the tire, which was not unduly worn and which still had many miles of wear in it. When I opened the trunk to get the jack, it wasn't there. I then decided to call the service station two blocks west across from East High School. Near my car on the south side of the street was the door to a small apartment, which was in the basement of the corner house. I decided to go there to ask to borrow the telephone to call the service station. A young woman answered the doorbell and graciously allowed me to use her phone. I noticed on entering the apartment that she seemed to be somewhat agitated. So, before leaving, I asked if there were anything I could do to help. She explained she was new in the neighborhood and wanted to talk to the bishop of the ward but she did not know who he was or how to get in touch with him. I then gave her the name of Merrill C. Faux, the bishop of the Yale First Ward, and got his address and telephone number from the directory for her use. She thanked me and I left, thinking nothing more about it.

A few days later, I attended a reception in the foyer of the Yale Ward chapel where Bishop Faux and his wife were in the receiving line. As I shook hands with Sister Faux, she said, "I understand you were the answer to a young woman's prayers." When I asked what she meant, she said that the young woman whose phone I borrowed had called the bishop. She explained she had recently moved into her apartment, was badly in need of help and had felt alone and isolated, not knowing who to turn to. During the afternoon before I rang her bell, she had been praying fervently for help and direction. She looked upon my arrival as a direct answer to her prayers and so informed the bishop when she met with him.

In reflecting on this incident, several questions have occurred to me: First, was it mere happenstance that the first and only loud blow out of my life occurred at that time and place while driving a luxury car (Cadillac) on a city street? I think not. I believe I was the instrument in God's hands to assist this young woman who needed help urgently and who had prayed to her Heavenly Father diligently and with faith. Second, were there not other persons or agencies than me who could have come to her aid? Certainly. But at that time of the afternoon and at that place, who would it have been? It is true, she could have asked a neighbor but the fact is she did not do so and instead asked her Heavenly Father who had instructed her—as He instructs us all—to come to Him when in need. Third, was there not some other way the Lord could have signaled me to ring that doorbell than to have made it mandatory that I do so in response to a personal need? Certainly. He could have spoken to me through the Spirit saying, "Stop here and go ring that door bell. Fourth, is it possible that He spoke to me in that manner but I was so pre-occupied and so inattentive to His whisperings that I did not hear? The answer, of course, is yes. And that to me is the most disturbing aspect of the incident.

CHAPTER FORTY-NINE

"The Opportunity to Serve"
by Daniel Bay Gibbons

One of the highlights of my life occurred in 1991, when I accompanied my father, Francis M. Gibbons, on a trip to Benson, Arizona. At the time, Dad was just concluding his service as a General Authority, and had an assignment to reorganize the stake presidency in the Benson Stake. Since Dad is a native son of Arizona, he suggested that the two of us take a week and drive down together, stopping en route to visit the place of his birth in St. Johns, and then on the return trip to visit Phoenix, where he had spent his teenage years.

This father-and-son road trip blessed my life in many ways. For example, we had many hours to engage in deep conversation about life, the gospel, our family, and the future. I also learned things about my father I had never known. For example, while driving through the Kaibab Plateau in Northern Arizona our conversation somehow turned to poetry. Dad recited to me the long poem, "Ulalume," by Edgar Allan Poe, which he told me he had committed to memory as a teenager in Phoenix. I was astounded in two respects: First, that my father had in his memory a poem learned in his youth, and second, that he had been fascinated by so dark and profound piece. I then recited a poem for Dad that I had memorized, I think "The Lake Isle of Innisfree" by William Butler Yeats, and it was Dad's turn to be astounded. We then, over a period of a couple of hours, unfolded for each other dozens of poems that we had each privately memorized as young men. It was a sweet experience.

During this trip we also talked often of Dad's father and my grandfather, Andrew Smith Gibbons, who was a superior court judge in Apache County, Arizona, during the early years of the last century. Even though I had never met this grandfather, who died young, seventeen years before my birth, I felt then and still feel now a deep kinship to him, largely through the stories my father told me about him.

But this trip was also the setting for one of the most profound spiritual experiences I have ever had, one that has had far-reaching impact on my life over the intervening twenty-three years.

When we arrived in Benson on Saturday morning, I drove Dad to the stake center, where he spent the entire day interviewing the bishops, high council members and others as part of the process of selecting a new stake president. Meantime, I drove to nearby Tombstone, Arizona, where I saw that fascinating old Wild West community where so much history had unfolded in the nineteenth century, and where later my grandfather had often appeared as a trial attorney and substitute judge. That evening I attended the adult session of stake conference and was called upon to bear my testimony. The next morning, Dad and I checked out of our hotel and attended the general session of the conference together, where Dad presented a new stake presidency. The new presidency was comprised of very young men of about my age, in their late twenties or early thirties. They were healthy, energetic, and filled with the spirit and fervor of their new responsibilities. As they spoke to their flock in the conference, I honestly felt a little envious of them, and of the grand adventure they were about to embark upon in their new ministry, and the opportunities they would have to serve. At the time I was serving as the second counselor in the elders quorum presidency in my home ward, and I felt passed over, underused and forgotten. Later, Dad invited me to sit in the room as he set these men apart. We then bid them adieu, got in our car, and drove away.

As we drove from Benson towards Phoenix, I made this comment to Dad: "I almost feel envious of those three men. It will be like another full-time mission for them."

"Now Dan," Dad responded. "You want to be very careful. You don't want to ever allow the seeds of aspiration to be planted in your heart."

I then told Dad that I wasn't envious because of the honor they had received with their new callings, but with the opportunity to serve which was before them.

Dad and I then had a long discussion about the blessings of Church service, as well as the almost universal danger of aspiring to callings. I shared with Dad my desires to give more service in the Church, and my feeling that I was underused in my current Church calling. Dad then made this powerful promise to me: "I promise you in the name of the Lord," he said, "that if you take your desire to serve to the Lord in prayer, He will open the way for you in a miraculous way."

I took this promise to heart, and through the remainder of the week, I commenced to pray with great focus and power for more opportunities to serve. I laid my soul out before the Lord and told Him that I didn't want Church position, only the blessing of giving service.

We returned home during the week, and the following Sunday I was astonished when Bishop C. Samuel Gustafson of the Cottonwood Third Ward pulled me aside after sacrament meeting and asked to speak with me. He told me about a confidential matter in the ward involving one of our members that he wanted my assistance with. At the time I was a practicing attorney, and over the succeeding months I spent countless hours with Bishop Gustafson counseling with this member and trying to find solutions to some thorny legal problems. None of the ward members ever knew about this anonymous service. It was essentially between the Lord, my bishop, and me, and I was so grateful to the Lord for the way He answered my prayer within seven days of my father giving me this special promise.

But the Lord wasn't finished! On Monday morning I was in my law office when the telephone rang. On the line was a woman from the Tolstoy Foundation's Refugee Resettlement Agency. She told me that there was a family from the former Soviet Union who were political refugees and that they would be coming to live in Salt Lake City in the next few days, and they needed a "sponsor" to help them get settled, find work, make friends, and adjust to life in the United States. Would I be their sponsor, she asked. My heart was pounding with gratitude to the Lord as I said, "Yes. Of course."

Thus began one of the most significant experiences in the life of our family. A few days later I found myself at a humble apartment near Salt Lake City's Liberty Park and met this family from Russia, comprised of a father and mother, a seven-year-old son, the parents of the father and an unmarried aunt of the father, so six members of one family in three generations. The young mother spoke a little English, and I spoke a very little Russian. I welcomed the family, and quickly took inventory of what they needed, which was basically everything, since they had left Russia with the clothes upon their backs and a few duffel bags of modest belongings. Within a day or two I had assembled from our home ward the donation of an entire station wagon full of household goods—pillows, blankets, sheets, towels, appliances, dishes, silverware, a television, food storage, etc. On the Saturday after their arrival I took three of my little girls, Annie, Jenny and Elizabeth, over to the home of my new Russian friends to unload all of the goods. They shed tears of joy as we took everything into the apartment.

When we were through unpacking, the young mother said to me in halting English, "Dan, we are Christians, and in our first Sunday in freedom, we would like to worship in a Christian church. Do you know where we can find a Christian church?"

I responded, "I'm a Christian, and you can come with me to my church." So the next day, two weeks after my father's remarkable prophecy, we brought our six new Russian friends to the Cottonwood Third Ward. I gave the family the Russian Bible I had purchased on my mission in Germany, as well as my copy of the newly translated Russian *Book of Mormon*. They attended the whole meeting block with us, and afterward came to our home for dinner. Thus began one of the sweetest associations of our lives. The younger three members of the family, the father mother and son, were all later baptized. Furthermore, it was from this experience that I once again dusted off the memory of spiritual yearnings I had received in the mission field to study Russian.

Now at the distance of almost a quarter of century from this remarkable prophecy of my father's, I marvel at the way the Lord blessed me through his ministry. What began as merely a prayer for more opportunities to serve resulted in our being better prepared, twenty years later, to serve a mission in Russia. I'm grateful to the Lord for this great blessing.

CHAPTER FIFTY

Finding a Lost Missionary
by Daniel Bay Gibbons

While serving as an assistant to President Hans-Juergen Saager in the Germany Duesseldorf Mission in 1978, I had a remarkable spiritual experience with my companion, Elder Kenneth Scott Morrell. President Saager's English language ability was limited, and so he often called upon his assistants to assist with missionaries in difficulty. President Saager had spent several hours one day counseling with a companionship of sister missionaries, then serving in the city of Gerresheim, Germany, who were having a personal conflict in their companionship. The next day the companionship problems erupted again, resulting in one of the sister missionaries running away from her companion. My missionary diary entry tells the rest of the story (with the names of the sisters omitted):

> After our lunch I received a telephone call from Sister X in Gerresheim. She told me that her companion, Sister Y, had left her alone in the apartment and fled on foot, threatening to return home. Elder Morrell and I had spent almost four hours yesterday in the office with President Saager, who counseled with these two sisters about their companionship problems. We conferred with President Saager, who asked us to drive to Gerresheim to try to find Sister Y. Elder Morrell and I said a prayer, and then departed in our car.

We drove to Gerresheim where we found Sister X alone, searching for her companion. After dropping Sister X off at her apartment to wait, Elder Morrell and I decided to look for Sister Y.

I testify that the Lord guides his prayerful servants, because in this city of 500,000 people, we were led directly to Sister Y within a period of about ten minutes. We got in the car and I drove down a random street in Gerresheim. We parked the car and walked one block, turned down a certain forest path in a city park, and found a crying Sister Y, sitting alone on a park bench with her suitcase. She had cooled off, and told us she was ready to return to her companion.

CHAPTER FIFTY-ONE

"The Church with the Long Name"

by Francis M. Gibbons

While on vacation in the coastal city of Santos, Brazil, Ernani Teixeira and his wife saw a church with a sign reading, "A Igreja de Jesus Cristo dos Santos dos Ultimos Dias." Afterward the couple joked about "the Church with the long name." However, as they returned to their home in Sao Paulo, Ernani and his wife could not stop thinking about "the church with the long name", and ultimately Ernani told his wife that they must return to Santos to visit the church. That very evening two missionaries from "the church with the long name" knocked on their apartment door in Sao Paulo.

Ernani Teixeira was born and raised in a small town in the interior of Brazil. He was born with clubfeet, a condition that was corrected over seven years by the use of heavy braces. During these years, therefore, he was unable to walk and play as other children. This gave him a meditative attitude and turned his mind toward the marvels of the earth and the heavenly bodies. Thus he began to wonder about God, the Creator, and about how He communicates with earthly beings. Ernani looks on this stressful period positively, as it first caused him to think about the need for prophets to reveal God's will.

While completing his undergraduate studies in economics at the university in Belo Horizonte, Ernani met and began dating his future wife, Gisa. They were married February 13, 1969, and later moved to Sao Paulo, where he began work on his M.A. program at the University.

Both Ernani and Gisa felt a lack in the church of their youth and began reading the Bible together to form a basis for their religious life. The New Testament accounts of the Savior's words and miracles created a sense of the reality of His existence and inspired them with the desire to find the Savior's true church, if it were on the earth. They began to pray to this end.

On a weekend holiday in Santos, a resort city on the beach, they passed a chapel with the sign "A Igreja de Jesus Cristo dos Santos dos Ultimos Dias" (The Church of Jesus Christ of Latter-day Saints). They remarked about the length of the name and wondered, in a humorous vein, whether they should investigate this Church with the long name.

On returning home, Ernani found the name of this church repeatedly coming to his mind, though it was not in connection with their recent holiday at the beach. It occurred even when he was in the midst of his studies. When he went home for lunch on the following Wednesday and told Gisa about the way in which the name of this church kept coming to his mind, he found that she too had been thinking about this church with the long name. "What shall we do now?" asked Gisa. "We have been praying for an answer." Ernani replied, "We need to check it out. Let's find out if there is such a church here in Sao Paulo. If not, next weekend we are going back to Santos." However, when he returned from the University that evening, he was astonished to hear Gisa say, "Two missionaries of that church knocked at our door this afternoon. Since you've been very busy in your program, I made an appointment for Saturday." Of the events that followed, Ernani wrote, "That was how it all started. How happy we were to find out and finally know for ourselves the Lord has restored His true Church and we are led by a true prophet. We were both baptized on 7 June 1969."

Soon after his baptism, Ernani received his patriarchal blessing and then was offered a scholarship from the United States government to attend the University of Southern California at Los Angeles on a Ph.D. program in economics. At first, Gisa was unable to join him because of a lack of housing near the UCLA campus. He lived in a dormitory and for the first week felt sad and isolated. He was then transferred to a room on the other side of the dormitory. "When I got there and looked through the window," he reported, "I saw the most beautiful view. There was the Los Angeles Temple. I could recognize it from a picture I had seen. I just dropped my suitcases and ran. When I saw the House of the Lord, I realized that I was not alone." Gisa joined him later and they were sealed in the Los Angeles Temple on November 3, 1971, about a month before their first child, Melissa, was born.

Several years later after Ernani had received his Ph.D. in economics, he was offered an alluring job with the International Monetary Fund. "That job would have been the fulfillment of a dream," he wrote, "if I had not received my patriarchal blessing indicating my place would be in Brazil and that I needed to serve the Lord." Acting on faith, Ernani declined the offer and he and Gisa returned to Belo Horizonte, Brazil, with no assurance of employment. Soon, however, he became a member of the faculty at the University and later became a full professor in economics.

Meanwhile, Ernani and Gisa were active in the small branch in Belo Horizonte, serving in many positions. The fact they were the only couple in the area who had been sealed in the temple placed them in a special position of leadership. Of course, after the Sao Paulo Temple was dedicated in the autumn of 1978, other couples there were sealed in the temple.

On February 15, 1981, Ernani Teixeira was sustained as the first president of the Belo Horizonte Brazil Stake. Six years later, he received an offer from UCLA to return for post-doctoral work, which would have greatly increased his professional standing. However, within the hour after making arrangements for a leave of absence from the university, on February 24, 1987, he received a call to serve as a Regional Representative of the Twelve. Once again he made the choice of serving where the Lord wanted him to serve. He was set apart to his new calling on April 6, 1987, in Salt Lake City during General Conference. Present on this occasion were Elder Kletting and Elder Weaver, the two missionaries who had taught the Teixeiras eighteen years earlier. Ernani reported, "We had a chance to read the journal of one of those two missionaries. They were fasting and also praying to find a family. They were led to our place in a miraculous way. It's amazing to know how the Lord leads our paths if we want to find the truth. We became witnesses that the Father really answers our prayers."

In 1995 Elder Teixeira was called as an Area Authority Seventy and sustained as a member of the Third Quorum of Seventy.

CHAPTER FIFTY-TWO

"Go See Bob, Now!"

by Daniel Bay Gibbons

One of the sweetest experiences of my service as a bishop occurred in January of 2000. One evening I was sitting with my wife, Julie, at a Young Women's basketball game for our ward when I felt a powerful impression that I should "Go see Bob!" Bob was a marvelous high priest in our ward, a veteran of World War II, a father, and a grandfather. Bob had also been struggling with cancer for several months and was the subject of frequent prayers in the Cottonwood Third Ward. As I received this clear impression, I thought to myself, "Yeah. That's a good idea. I'll go see Bob later this week."

The game continued, and after a few minutes I again had the impression, "Go see Bob!" My thought then was, "Yes. I really need to go see Bob tonight after the game."

I continued to watch the girls play ball, but the impression came a third time, but much stronger, "Go see Bob, now!"

I heeded the prompting, stood up, told Julie that I needed to leave, and walked out during the middle of the game.

When I arrived at Bob's house I found that he was in physical distress, and I went right to his bedside, where I stood next to Mary, his wife of fifty years. I took Bob by the hand, and told him I loved him. He smiled at me, and squeezed my hand. I then stood there holding Bob by the hand while speaking quietly with Mary.

Within a minute or two of my arrival, Bob died. I was literally holding his hand and wrist when he slipped away, and I felt his pulse stop.

Throughout the evening and in the coming days I was able to be of significant comfort and blessing to this family, who were not all, at that time, strong in the faith. I helped call family members, confer with the mortuary, discuss funeral arrangements, and gathered the family around Bob's bedside for a final kneeling family prayer. It was a sad, but very sweet, evening.

Shortly after Bob's death, his daughter, who had also been present the night of his death, returned to Church for the first time in twenty-five years and later qualified to receive a temple recommend from me. Later, Bob's grandniece took the missionary lessons in our home during the summer of 2001, and then asked me to baptize her, which I did. I believe that witnessing the teaching of this young woman by the full-time missionaries in our home and her baptism was one of the great spiritual experiences in the lives of our children and helped to prepare our Annie, Liz, and Josh for their future calls to the mission field. Finally, the granddaughter of the deceased also sought my counsel, returned to activity in the Church, and in 2002 asked me to bless her firstborn son, Bob's great-grandson.

I am so grateful for the thrice-repeated impression to leave a basketball game and visit Bob. It has been a great blessing in my life, in the lives of Bob's family, and especially in the lives of my family.

CHAPTER FIFTY-THREE

"That Man Needs a Blessing"

by Daniel Bay Gibbons

One day sitting on the stand in sacrament meeting, while serving as bishop of the Cottonwood Third Ward, I was looking into the faces of my ward members, and I had the strong impression that a particular brother needed a blessing. This man was a stalwart high priest, a temple recommend holder and a returned missionary of about sixty years of age. I had my executive secretary invite this man to see me in the bishop's office later in the day.

When the man came in I told him, "I don't know why you are here, other than I have the impression that you may need a blessing." He was silent for a long moment, and tears came to his eyes. He finally said that it was amazing that I should have sought him out, because he had never received a patriarchal blessing. Somehow he had been ordained to all of the offices of the Aaronic Priesthood as a boy, prepared for a mission, received a mission call, received his endowment in the temple, served a great mission, married, had a family and served in the Church over many decades without ever receiving a patriarchal blessing. He told me that within the past few days he had been troubled by the fact that he had never received his blessing, and had received several promptings that he ought to seek one out despite the fact that he was much older than most recipients of patriarchal blessings.

I immediately interviewed this good brother and gave him a recommend to receive his patriarchal blessing, which he did a few days later.

This experience was a great testimony to me that the Lord is aware of us and aware of our needs, and is ready to inspire His servants to be instruments in His hands for the blessing of his children.

CHAPTER FIFTY-FOUR

"Talk to That Man"

by Francis M. Gibbons

During my service in Brazil, I attended a conference in the Ponta Grossa Stake. During the general session Sunday morning, I saw a man in the audience who seemed pre-occupied and unhappy and who failed to vote one way or the other as to one of the stake officers. As I sat on the stand, the Spirit whispered to me "Talk to that man." After the meeting, I sought him out. His name was Luiz Kulchetschi. We sat together in a corner of the chapel where I spent some time talking to him. He was a fine, intelligent-looking man who, I learned, taught at one of the colleges in the city. I also learned that he had had a misunderstanding with a certain man in the stake presidency, and that he had once served on the high council but apparently had asked for a release because of the bad feelings which had been generated by the misunderstanding. I endeavored as best I could to moderate those feelings, expressed my love for him, and told him I was his friend and that if he needed me I was available to help.

Later he came to Sao Paulo to see me to seek counsel about furthering his education in Canada. I encouraged him to try to do it if he could see his way clear. I later received a long letter from Luiz, written on the letterhead of the School of Forestry at a university in Edmonton, Canada. In it, he described the success he and his family are having there, that he has done excellent work in his studies and that he was going on to Calgary to complete them at a university there. He said he was at peace with himself and expressed thanks for the time I had taken to talk to and to listen to him at the stake conference in Ponta Grossa, indicating that it had had a powerful influence for good in his life.

I am grateful to the Lord that I was able to help this brother and pray that I will have the Spirit of the Lord to be with me always to help guide and prompt me in all things, all times, and in all places so that I can be an instrument for good during all my days.

CHAPTER FIFTY-FIVE

"For the Prisoners Shall Go Free"

by Daniel Bay Gibbons

In the 1990's I served for nearly four years as a counselor to elders quorum president Michael J. Lundberg. The other counselor was J. Scott Riches, and the three of us felt as if we were young missionaries once more as we ministered to our quorum, visiting, teaching, challenging, and helping. In 1991, I had this remarkable spiritual experience while visiting, which recalled many experiences of the mission field:

> One evening I was visiting in the ward with Scott Riches. As we drove through the neighborhood, I had a strong and clear impression that we should drop in on a single mother with four or five young children. We knocked on the door and sat down in the living room to visit with this sister while her children prepared for bed. A few minutes after we arrived, there was another knock at the door. It was a constable who had a warrant for this woman's arrest on a misdemeanor traffic matter. The constable told her that it was his duty to book her into jail unless she could post bail. Moreover, the officer stated that if she were booked into jail that her children would have to be placed in the custody of the State. The woman burst into tears, as she had no money to post the bail.

I asked the officer if he would give me a few moments, whereupon I returned home, got my checkbook, and posted bail for her in a fairly nominal amount. Afterwards, Scott and I expressed gratitude that we heeded the impression to knock on this particular door on this particular night, and were thus able to be in the right place at the right time to help this poor sister. It reminded me of this great description of the atonement of Christ, which gives us "that which would enable us to redeem them out of their prison, for the prisoners shall go free!" (D&C 128:22—this, by the way, is the favorite scripture of my companion, Scott Riches)

CHAPTER FIFTY-SIX

A Cry for Help

by Daniel Bay Gibbons

While attending law school in Oregon from 1983 to 1986, I was called as the elders quorum president in the Keizer First Ward. I had a large and diverse quorum of elders, including many inactive brethren. Julie and I lived in a modest apartment located along a busy road. In one direction was the law school. In the other direction was the church building. Between these two poles I tried to carefully balance my life. Though I was very busy with my studies and as a husband and father of two small girls, Annie and Jenny, I focused as much attention to my church calling as I could.

One of my quorum members was a Vietnam veteran who had suffered significant injuries during the war and was a paraplegic, confined to a wheelchair. He was a good man, suffering through a difficult time. Though he did not attend church, nor adhere to the Word of Wisdom or other standards, his testimony was deep. This diary entry of January 20, 1985, recounts an experience with this man:

> I had a faith-promoting experience last night before I retired to sleep. As I was kneeling in prayer, I heard the voice of a man crying repeatedly for help. I looked through the window, but could see no one, so I dressed and went outside to investigate. I saw a light across the street and heard the cries for help again. I called in answer and walked to the light and found one of my prospective elders, a paraplegic, trapped in his wheelchair

in a muddy hole, unable to extricate himself, intoxicated, and freezing without a coat or wrap. He recognized me and apologized for his drunken state as I pulled him out of his fix. I accompanied him the half-mile or so to his house, pushing him up the steep inclines, as the batteries on his self-propelled chair were low. I left him in the charge of his wife at their door. I count it a blessing of the Lord that I, as his quorum president, was awake and able to hear and respond to his cries. This man remarked to me that no one seemed to care enough to respond to his pleas. I thank the Lord that I was able to hear and respond.

This experience seems to me to capture the essence of missionary work and the work of the priesthood.

CHAPTER FIFTY-SEVEN

"A Distinct Impression to Stop and Knock"

by Daniel Bay Gibbons

One day in the Spring of 2000, while serving as the bishop of the Cottonwood Third Ward in Holladay, Utah, I was driving down a street in my ward when I had a distinct impression to stop and knock on a particular door. I ignored the prompting and drove on. That evening, I drove by the house again with my family on the way to a school function with our children. Again, I had a distinct impression to stop and knock, but with my children in the car I ignored the impression. The following morning as I drove past the house on my way to work, the prompting came again to stop and knock, but with greater clarity and urgency. I turned the car around at the end of the block and drove back.

I approached the house not knowing exactly what I should say. I stood on the doorstep and knocked. A young woman answered the door with a baby in her arms. I introduced myself as her neighbor and the bishop of the local LDS ward and asked her if there was anything I could do for her. She said, "Yes, maybe you can help me." She then explained that her father had recently died in California, that she had just returned home from the funeral, and that she was having a hard time dealing with his death. She then said,

"It's really strange that you would come by today, because just this morning I told my husband that maybe I ought to go to a church or talk to someone from a church."

In the following few months this woman was taught all of the missionary discussions by the full-time missionaries, and in September of 2000 she asked me to baptize her, which I did.

Part Seven

"THERE'S SURELY SOMEWHERE A LOWLY PLACE"

There's sure somewhere a lowly place
In earth's harvest fields so wide
Where I may labor through life's short day
For Jesus, the Crucified.
So trusting my all to thy tender care,
And knowing thou lovest me,
I'll do thy will with a heart sincere:
I'll be what you want me to be?

—Hymn 270, Verse 3

CHAPTER FIFTY-EIGHT

"Sir, How Long Must We Wait?"
by Daniel Bay Gibbons

n the early 1960's, two sister missionaries serving in London, England, gave a Book of Mormon and other Church literature to their landlady and taught her the missionary discussions, only to hear that she was not interested in their message. Little did the missionaries know that they had planted a seed of the gospel that would result in the conversion of hundreds of souls in Ghana, Africa.

In the early 1960's, a Dr. Mensa from Ghana, West Africa, went to live for a time in London, England. While he was there, the landlady of his London flat, knowing that Dr. Mensa wished to improve his English, gave him some books written in English. Among the books was a copy of *The Book of Mormon* and other LDS literature. These materials had been given to the landlady some time before by two sister missionaries from the United States. The missionaries had taught the landlady the discussions, only to have the landlady say that she was not interested in the gospel.

Dr. Mensa returned to Ghana, taking *The Book of Mormon* with him. Ultimately he gave it to a friend of his, Joseph William Billy Johnson, a native of the Cape Coast area of Ghana. Joseph William Billy Johnson was converted after prayerfully studying *The Book of Mormon*. A short time after his spiritual conversion, Joseph had a remarkable experience. He reports:

[O]ne early morning, while about to prepare for my daily work, I saw the heavens open and angels with trumpets singing songs of praise unto God. I heard my name mentioned thrice: "Johnson, Johnson, Johnson. If you will take up my work as I will command you, I will bless you and bless your land." Trembling and in tears, I replied, "Lord, with thy help, I will do whatever you will command me." From that day onward, I was constrained by the Spirit to go from street to street to deliver the message that we read from the Book of Mormon.

Joseph thus embarked on a personal "mission" to spread the message of *The Book of Mormon*.

Between 1964 and 1978, Joseph was instrumental in converting hundreds of residents of the Cape Coast area to the truth of *The Book of Mormon*. On behalf of these converts, Joseph sought more information about the Church by corresponding with Church headquarters. Books were sent to Ghana from Salt Lake City. Joseph and others made many direct appeals to the First Presidency of the Church. In the years leading up to the momentous events of 1978, Joseph wrote several times to President Spencer W. Kimball imploring him to send missionaries. In one especially heartfelt letter, he stated emphatically to President Kimball, "Sir. How long must we wait?"

Joseph and the other early converts in Ghana met together in church services and strived to live by the teachings of the gospel as contained in *The Book of Mormon*, the *Doctrine and Covenants* and the teachings of the prophets. Without the benefit of priesthood authority or ordinances, entire congregations were organized in Ghana. A similar phenomenon occurred in neighboring Nigeria.

In June of 1978, the First Presidency announced a revelation, far-reaching in its impact, extending the priesthood to all worthy male Church members without regard for race or color. Joseph's sincere pleas to President Kimball had been answered.

A few months after the announcement, the first official representatives of the Church, two mature missionary couples, were sent to West Africa by the First Presidency. These missionaries, Edwin Q. and Janath Cannon and Rendell N. and Rachel Mabey, made contact with the many "Mormon" congregations then meeting and worshiping in Ghana and Nigeria. A third missionary couple joined the Cannons and the Mabeys within a few months. They performed the first officially recognized baptisms in West Africa in Ghana on Nov. 21, 1978, including the baptisms of Joseph W. B. Johnson and dozens of others who belonged to congregations set up by Joseph. Within a few months, these six missionaries oversaw some 1,700 baptisms in West Africa. Joseph became a faithful member of the Church, ultimately serving as a patriarch in the Cape Coast Stake in Ghana.

The two sister missionaries who labored in London in the early 1960's would have little suspected the remarkable impact they had by placing a Book of Mormon with their landlady. "Out of small things proceedeth that which is great." (D&C 64:33).

CHAPTER FIFTY-NINE

Destitute of Everything Except Faith

by Francis M. Gibbons

arl Christian Anthon Christensen, an artist trained at the Royal Academy of Fine Arts in Copenhagen, Denmark, abandoned a promising career as a painter when he joined the Church in 1853. Arriving in Utah "destitute of everything except faith," he soon began work on an epic series of paintings, the "Mormon Panorama," which have become among the most widely seen and admired art to the come out of the Church in the nineteenth century.

Carl Christian Anthon Christensen was born in Copenhagen, Denmark, on November 28, 1831. He was converted to The Church of Jesus Christ of Latter-day Saints at age nineteen and was baptized September 26, 1850. From early youth, Carl showed exceptional artistic talent. Encouraged by family and friends, he enrolled in the Royal Academy of Fine Arts in Copenhagen. There his native talents were cultivated and channeled, equipping him with skills which were to create enjoyment for himself and others and provide a means of livelihood for his family.

Once Carl Christensen joined the Mormon church, however, his artistic skills were relegated to a place of minor importance in his life. The precepts and the mission of his adopted religion then became the primary focus of his daily activity and the motivating force that propelled him along. That bias became evident not long after his conversion when, in January 1853, he was called to serve a short-term mission in an area south of Copenhagen. Elder Christensen proved to be an effective missionary whose spiritual qualities and zeal helped lead many into the Church. So successful was he on this his first mission, and so willing was he to serve, that in October 1853, only three months after his release, he was called on a second mission and assigned to labor in Norway. Sailing up the Kattegat and across the Skagerrak, Elder Christensen entered a country whose language and customs were strange and whose officials generally frowned upon Mormon missionaries. He was jailed twice in Drammen for preaching on the streets, and in other places was shunned and looked on with suspicion. However, the reception in Christiania was better, and there, with his companion, he was able to build up a branch. Here Elder Christensen also worked part time as a painter to acquire the means to continue with his mission. He also did this in Frederikstad, Norway, and in other Norwegian cities.

After serving eighteen months, he was released; but in September 1855, only a few months after returning home, he was called to serve again in Norway. This time, succeeding Canute Peterson, Elder Christensen presided over the entire country of Norway.

On returning home from this his third mission in April 1857, Carl decided to immigrate to the United States in order to join the main body of the Saints. In Liverpool, England, while awaiting transport, he met and courted a young convert, Elise Haarly, who also was immigrating to America. They were married in Liverpool before their ship embarked. To help defray expenses, Carl served as a steward aboard ship. He was also a division captain of their handcart company, which crossed the plains in the late summer of 1857. The young couple arrived in Salt Lake City on September 13, 1857, "destitute of everything except faith in God and the hope of better days."

At first, Carl accepted any work that was available. He worked as a wood carrier and charcoal bearer. Later he did farming and house painting. Finally he began to do painting, which reflected his artistic skill. He was employed to paint scenes for the Salt Lake Theatre. Later he painted murals in the St. George and Manti Temples. Meanwhile, he was engaged in creating a wide variety of historical and genre paintings. He received premium awards for paintings displayed at various art fairs. And his "Mormon Panorama" is regarded as "the most significant series of LDS historical paintings from the nineteenth century." It includes "twenty-three tempera paintings, each six feet by ten feet, recounting the pre-Utah history of the church in epic dimensions." These paintings have been widely published and exhibited.

During the years Elder Christensen was creating this body of artistic work, he continued to work faithfully in the Church. From 1865-1868 and from 1887-1889 he served other missions in Scandinavia. During this last mission, he served as a writer and translator in the mission office in Copenhagen. Later he was employed in the Church Historian's office, compiling material for a history of the Scandinavian Mission. He became widely known in America and in Europe for his poetic and prose compositions. The Church hymnbook in Danish contains many lyrics he composed; and for twenty-six years he contributed to *Bikenben*, the Church publication in the Danish and Norwegian languages in America.

In March 1900, Elder Christensen was ordained a high priest and a patriarch by Elder Francis M. Lyman of the Twelve. During the remaining twelve years of his life, this benign, dignified, gentle man inspired and motivated many through the patriarchal blessings he conferred, blessings which reflected his own deep feelings about the Church and his love for the Savior.

CHAPTER SIXTY

"A Sack of Coal for Christmas"
by Daniel Bay Gibbons

A sack of coal, a newborn babe and a strange fire in the winter sky transformed my coldest, dreariest Christmas into a celebration of warmth and illumination.

I was called to serve in the Germany Duesseldorf Mission in 1976 and arrived in the field in late October. Only two days before Christmas, my companion, Elder Kerry Jon Williams, and I had been evicted from our snug little apartment in Duisburg, Germany, and forced to find new lodgings. We lived in a rough, working-class neighborhood in the heart of Europe's greatest industrial area, and housing was scarce. In desperation, we leased some unheated rooms almost in the shadow of the smokestacks of the vast Thyssen steel works. Early on the morning of Christmas Eve, I awoke in the darkness of a strange room, shivering beneath two tattered blankets, afraid to move for fear of losing the tenuous pocket of warmth around my body. The room was bitterly cold, the furniture Spartan, the walls unadorned. I lay watching the moonlight streaming through the uncurtained windows. Outside, the bare branches of the sycamore trees seemed to float above the heavy fog. Beyond loomed the shadowy silhouette of the steel plant. Suddenly a great ball of orange flame surged up from the largest smokestack, illuminating the sky, rivaling a sunset in color and intensity. I heard a distant roar, like Niagara, as the fireball danced and rolled on the horizon. Just as suddenly, the flame was extinguished and all was quiet.

I arose now from my bed, sat in a sagging armchair, and wrapped my blankets around me. Remembering that it was Christmas Eve, my first away from home, I tried to picture our house in Salt Lake City filled with warmth and light and the scent of pine. I thought of the lavish gifts under the tree, of my father wearing his red sweater, of my mother's baking, of visits from family and friends. My eyes suddenly brimmed over with tears as I contemplated a Christmas to be spent in the shadow of those smokestacks, surrounded by strangers, without a tree, without lights and gifts, without even a fire to chase away the chill December air.

Later in the day, my companion and I sat hunched in our overcoats, eating canned stew and bread, our breath rising in the little kitchen like great drafts of steam. A knock came at our door. I opened up to find a tall, thin figure dressed in boots, a threadbare coat, a red scarf, and a stocking cap. His black beard glistened with raindrops and his face was smudged with coal dust. It was Ude, a member of our little branch, a man of few words whom we barely knew. He was a refugee from East Germany who had married an Italian wife here in the west. Behind Ude was one of his friends, a thickset man with curly hair. They were both covered in coal dust, from their blackened boots to their darkened but smiling faces. They stood beside a rusty coal stove, which they had muscled up six flights of stairs. Without speaking, they dragged the stove over our threshold and into the corner of our sitting room, banging as they went, where they hooked it up to the stovepipe in the ceiling. Then they disappeared back down the stairs, only to return carrying two huge sacks of coal and a bundle of kindling.

The sweat ran in streaks down their smudged faces as they dropped the sacks in the corner. Ude turned to us and said, "Merry Christmas, brothers. These are your presents! One sack for each of you." We laughed with them at the strange gifts. Ude's friend bent to stack kindling in the belly of the stove. He struck a match and stepped back as the kindling smoked and then flamed up. He adjusted the damper, threw on more wood, and finally fed in the glossy lumps of precious coal. We crowded around, warming our hands before the flames. The metal ticked and creaked as the old structure heated up. Soon a delicious heat rolled off the stove in waves to fill our room. Ude and his friend stood up to leave. "I'll be back to pick you up at 6:00," he said at the door.

That evening Ude drove us to his apartment in his old compact car. His quiet, dark-haired wife met us at the door, beaming and holding their newborn son in a basket. We sat down by the fire. Ude and his wife moved around the tiny apartment, carrying food to the table. The baby stirred in his basket and Ude's wife came and laid him in my arms. He awoke and gazed up at me, the candlelight reflecting in his dark eyes. As I watched the little boy, I thought of another Christmas, long ago, when a young man and his wife found only cold lodgings for their newborn son. They too, had received unusual gifts from strangers and had seen a new star in the sky. I rocked the little boy as he babbled and reached and kicked his legs.

The next morning I again awoke early. The room was warm, the Christmas coal still glowing in the stove. I went to the window and gazed out through the frosted glass. A dusting of snow covered every stone and branch. The great smokestacks towered up darkly in the distance. As I watched, the orange flame surged up again into the night like a great star. Again I thought of my home far away, and of the bright lights and gifts under the Christmas tree. But it occurred to me that had I been home for Christmas I may never have received a gift of coal, or rocked a newborn babe, or seen His star in the sky.

CHAPTER SIXTY-ONE

"I've Planted Thirteen Orchards"

by Daniel Bay Gibbons

A member of the first company of pioneers to enter the Salt Lake Valley, Andrew Smith Gibbons assisted in settling Salt Lake City, Bountiful, Lehi, Cedar City, St. George, and at least eight other Mormon settlements in the West. In every place that he settled, he planted a peach orchard.

Andrew Smith Gibbons had a twin brother named Richard. Sons of William Davidson Gibbons, their mother, Mary (Polly) Hoover Gibbons, died soon after their birth, on March 21, 1825. As the father had four other young children to care for, and because of the need of nursing mothers for the twins, Andrew was taken into the family of Joshua Smith and his wife Sarah. Richard was given to a family named Caninne. Since the father, William Davidson Gibbons, died soon after, Andrew never knew his natural parents. And because he had been nurtured with love throughout his growing up years by Joshua and Sarah Smith, he took the name Smith as his middle name in honor of his adoptive parents.

Andrew was introduced to The Church of Jesus Christ of Latter-day Saints in 1836 when the Smith family moved to Kirtland, Ohio. Their purpose in moving there was to be near the Prophet Joseph Smith and other leaders of the church. This was the year in which the Kirtland Temple was dedicated, a time when there was such a rich spiritual outpouring among the Latter-day Saints. As Andrew mingled with the young people in Kirtland, he unknowingly became part of the first youth group in the first ward of the restored Church.

From this time, Andrew Smith Gibbons' life became inextricably entwined with the Mormon church. Migrating from Ohio to Missouri to Illinois as the pressures on the Church and its members dictated, Andrew and the Joshua Smith family became settled in Nauvoo, Illinois. The Smith home in Nauvoo was located near the home of Vinson Knight, who was the bishop of the lower ward. Here Andrew became acquainted with one of the bishop's daughters, Rizpah Knight, to whom he was married in the Nauvoo Temple on January 5, 1846. Soon afterward, the newlyweds joined the Mormon Exodus from Nauvoo, migrating to Winter Quarters, Nebraska, in company with Rizpah's mother, Martha, and other members of her family. Martha, whose husband, Bishop Vinson Knight, died in 1842, was later married to the Prophet Joseph Smith; and after his martyrdom she was married to Heber C. Kimball for time only.

When the personnel for the advance Mormon pioneer company was being drawn up in the spring of 1847, President Brigham Young selected twenty-two-year-old Andrew Smith Gibbons as a member. The Prophet, whose Nauvoo home was adjacent to the home of Bishop Vinson Knight, was well acquainted with young Andrew, whose work as a stevedore on the Mississippi Riverboats had toughened his muscular body so as to make him an apt candidate for the pioneer company. He was assigned to the gun division. After arriving in the Salt Lake Valley on July 24, 1847, with the pioneer company, Andrew helped build cabins, plow the sun-baked soil, and plant a crop before returning to Winter Quarters later that year. Then in 1852 he returned to Utah with Rizpah and their three oldest children who had been born in the Mormon villages at the Missouri River.

Then followed a series of nomadic moves for the Gibbons family, always at the direction of Church leaders. They settled first in Bountiful, Utah, then in Lehi, Utah, then in Cedar City, Utah, then in St. George and Santa Clara, Utah, where Andrew became the first sheriff of Washington County. He also began service there as an Indian missionary, a work in which he was engaged for over twenty-five years. He learned several Indian dialects and occasionally served as a translator for the leading brethren who travelled into Southern Utah and Northern Arizona. He was with the first group of missionaries who crossed the Colorado River in 1857 to work with the Hopi Indians at Old Oraibi. He and three companions remained to live and work with the Hopis for a time.

Later, Andrew was called to settle at St. Thomas on the Muddy River, in what is now Nevada, where he continued to work with the Indians. This area was then thought to be part of Arizona. In 1869, he was elected to the Arizona Territorial Legislature. He and a companion, Octavius Gass, built a fourteen-foot boat, which they put in the Colorado River and floated in to Yuma, Arizona. From there they took a stage across the desert to Tucson, Arizona, then the territorial capitol. When the session ended, Gass went east, and Andrew bought a horse and travelled alone over the five hundred miles from Tucson to St. Thomas. It was found later that St. Thomas was part of Nevada, which then levied back taxes on the saints living there. Unable to pay, the entire St. Thomas Ward, of which Andrew was a counselor in the bishopric, moved en masse to Long Valley, Utah, later named Glendale, after Bishop James Leithead's home in Scotland. Andrew's last call was to help settle the Mormon village in St. Johns, Arizona. He was the senior member of the high council there. With two others, he helped drive 450 head of cattle from Southern Utah to St. Johns to pay the balance on the purchase price of the town site. He grew one of the first orchards in the village, an activity that was typical of his pioneering. He often carried seeds in his saddlebags and planted them where he could find congenial soil. Near the end of his life, he called his youngest son, Leroy, to his side and, extending two peaches he had picked from his orchard toward him, said, "Since I came to Utah with the 1847 pioneers, I have put out thirteen orchards, and I have never eaten the fruit from any of them until now."

Leroy was next to the youngest of eighteen children, only seven of whom lived to maturity. Three of them died in one tragic night while the family lived in Glendale, Utah. In addition to the constant exertions of caring for her large family, Rizpah was a skilled midwife who was much in demand in the many pioneer communities where she lived.

Both Andrew and Rizpah died in St. Johns, he on February 9, 1886, and she on March 17, 1895. They were buried in the barren, wind-swept cemetery on the bluff overlooking St. Johns, far removed from the greenery of Ohio where they first met. Motivation for the long and perilous journey, a journey filled with both joy and anguish, was kindled by their convictions about the divine origins of The Church of Jesus Christ of Latter-day Saints.

CHAPTER SIXTY-TWO

The Family in the Last Farmhouse

by Francis M. Gibbons

n 1948 two missionaries were tracting in a rural area of Brazil when darkness began to fall. One of the missionaries, Elder Elmo Turner, suggested that they knock on the door of one last farmhouse. Inside they found the Brassanini family waiting for them—Mother Brassanini having had a vivid dream preparing the way for the missionaries' visit. One of the young children in the family was Pedro Brassanini, who became one of the great stalwarts of the kingdom in Brazil over the succeeding fifty years.

Joinville, Brazil, has the aspect of a German city. Its buildings and streets resemble many cities in the heart of European Germany. It is not uncommon to hear the German language spoken on its streets along with Portuguese, the national language of Brazil. When The Church of Jesus Christ of Latter-day Saints began to proselytize actively in Brazil in the 1930's and 1940's, the missionaries sent there worked chiefly among those who spoke German. So when a branch of the Church was built up in Joinville, one of the first LDS branches in all of Brazil, its meetings were conducted in the German language.

The Brassaninis were the first Portuguese-speaking family to attend the Joinville Branch. Father Brassanini operated a small farm several miles from the city. In 1948 two LDS missionaries were tracting in the country near the Brassanini farm. As the afternoon began to fade, one Elder suggested they suspend their work and return to the city so they could arrive before dark. The other, however, Elder Elmo Turner, suggested that they tract out one last farmhouse, just down the lane. The woman who answered the door, Mother Brassanini, greeted them with warmth and invited them in. She explained she had previously had a vivid dream in which she saw two young men who looked exactly like these two elders. She had been expecting them ever since. Not long after this first visit, the large Brassanini family was brought into the Church by Elder Elmo Turner and his companion.

It was not easy to integrate this family into the Joinville Branch. The long distance from the chapel and the language problem were not the only barriers. This farm family was poor compared to city dwellers, so poor, indeed, that the young Brassanini twins, Pedro and Paulo, did not have shoes. The father felt it was inappropriate to enter the chapel without shoes; so the twins were not allowed to attend meetings until money could be saved to buy them shoes. The first Sunday after the shoes were bought, Pedro and Paulo proudly wore them as they trudged into Joinville. Yet when they arrived at the chapel, their feet, which were unaccustomed to the tight confinement of shoes, were so swollen and blistered that Father Brassanini allowed the twins to remove their shoes as they entered the chapel!

The time came when Pedro was found worthy to serve and was called to serve as a missionary for the Church. But he lacked means to pay for his transportation to mission headquarters in Sao Paulo. As Father Brassanini was penniless, he suggested that Pedro ask farmers in the area for a loan. All turned him down except one who loaned him the money because he said he knew his father was an honest man.

In Sao Paulo, arrangements were made for Elder Pedro Brassanini to receive help from a priesthood quorum in Arizona to enable him to complete his mission. He served faithfully and effectively. His service was recognized by the call to serve as a district president. A highlight of his mission was the privilege of translating for President Henry D. Moyle at street meetings during President Moyle's brief visit in Brazil.

Elder Brassanini later filled a building mission, helping to construct chapels in the United States. To assist him with the language, he studied English briefly at Ricks College in Idaho. There he met Betty Norris, an Idaho native, whom he would marry years later after she had served a mission in Brazil under President Elmo Turner, the missionary who had taught the Brassanini family.

While working on the construction of a chapel, Pedro stayed in the homes of members. As he helped construct a chapel on the west side of the Salt Lake Valley, he was introduced to American humor. At the time he was living in the home of a family named Winder. One afternoon while at work, Pedro heard a helicopter overhead then a voice through a megaphone, which said ominously, "Pedro Brassanini, we are watching you." Being new to the country, he did not know but that he was under police surveillance. He learned later the voice belonged to Ned Winder who was taking aerial pictures for a business brochure the Winder family was preparing.

After Brother Brassanini's marriage to Betty Norris and after completing his education at the Brigham Young University, he was employed by the Church Education System. He taught seminary for a while on an Indian Reservation in Arizona. Later he transferred within the system to Brazil. While serving in Curitiba, he was called to preside over the Brazil Porto Alegre South Mission. And upon his release, he was called as a stake president in Curitiba. In 2006 he was called as president of the Porto Alegre Brazil Temple, with Sister Brassanini as temple matron.

With their bilingual abilities, the Brassaninis render significant service to the Church in Pedro's native land. His struggling years in poverty at Joinville are never far from his mind. And these memories enable him to see beyond the poverties of the moment, which affect many Brazilians, to times in the future when the miracle of the gospel plan will help lift thousands into a better life, as it helped him.

CHAPTER SIXTY-THREE

Miracle at Minus Forty
by Daniel Bay Gibbons

anuary in Siberia is not the optimum time or place for young missionaries to share the gospel on the street. The sun sets by mid-afternoon, and the temperatures can plummet to below minus forty degrees Fahrenheit for weeks at a time. The cold Arctic wind can literally be fatal within a few minutes without proper clothing or shelter. In this circumstance, President Gary Browning of the Moscow Russia Mission had counseled his missionaries during the extreme winter of 1993 to 1994 for safety purposes to avoid being out on the streets at night. One evening in January of 1994, Elders Ringger and Couch, two of the first missionaries to labor in the city of Novosibirsk, in Russian Siberia, were studying in their apartment, heedful of their mission president's instructions. But as the elders studied, they felt an overwhelming desire to go out on the street to find someone to teach. They knelt down together in the apartment to pray, and the Spirit whispered to them to go outside and preach! They put on their boots, coats, and Russian fur hats, and went out into the frigid night. There were few people on the street, and those who passed by were too cold to talk. Finally the Elders saw a man and woman of modest stature approaching them. It was to be a crucial moment in the history of the Church in Siberia.

Yuriy and Natasha Gushchin were both natives of Novosibirsk, the great Russian city built at the site of the railroad bridge over the Ob River. During the time of the Russian Empire, Novosibirsk was deemed to be the geographical center of Russia, and a small Church dedicated to St. Nicholas is found in the center of the city. It is also the largest city in Siberia, a vast region covering seven time zones and extending from Kazakhstan, China, and Mongolia northward far beyond the Arctic Circle. It is a place of beautiful landscape, extreme weather, and many large cities built during the time of the Russian Empire and the Soviet Union, Novosibirsk being the largest with a population of nearly two million people.

The year 1994 was a difficult time for the Gushchins, as it was for most other families of Russia. They lived in a modest apartment in the city and had a young daughter. Food was sometimes scarce, and the transition from a communist to a free market economy following the collapse of the Soviet Union created great challenges for ordinary Russian people.

On a bitterly cold Tuesday evening in January of 1994, Yuriy and Natasha returned home sadly, as they were worried about having enough money for food. There were few people about, as the temperature had plunged below minus forty degrees. As they walked through the deserted streets, they saw two young men up ahead. To their surprise, the young men stopped them and introduced themselves as missionaries of The Church of Jesus Christ. Yuriy said one of the missionaries, Elder Ringger, wore glasses, which were iced over in the cold, and that he tried to smile, but that his face was almost frozen in the cold. The hearts of Yuriy and Natasha went out to the two young American missionaries.

"We were attracted to their kindly faces. A light seemed to radiate out from them. We instantly felt tenderness toward them and invited them to our home." The elders asked if they could share a message about Jesus Christ, which they did.

After a few meetings with the elders, the Gushchins began to pray and quickly obtained testimonies about the truth of *The Book of Mormon*. Shortly thereafter, they also attended their first sacrament meeting. Despite the fact that the room rented for Church meetings was undergoing remodeling, the Gushchins felt immediately at home. "We loved being in Church," Yuriy later said. "We were surrounded by love! There were only six missionaries and two members in attendance, but incredible love was there, even though the facilities were imperfect. We both knew that there was something there. When the two hours of meetings were over, Natasha and I went outside and walked in silence for several minutes. Then I turned to her and said, 'I want to go back next week. This is the place!' Natasha then said to me, 'I think the same thing.'"

On May 8, 1994, Yuriy was baptized in the Ob River by Elder Ringger, and on June 23 it was his privilege to baptize his wife, as he had received the office of priest in the Aaronic Priesthood by that time.

Thus began their acquaintance with the missionaries, the Church, the holy scriptures, and with all of the gifts and blessings of our Heavenly Father. Out of that conversation on the street at minus forty degrees, they came to know *The Book of Mormon* is true and about the plan of salvation through the atonement of Jesus Christ. With each visit with the missionaries and in Church, hope sprang anew in their hearts and in their home—a hope that has never abandoned them.

In April of 2012, Yuriy Gushchin was sustained as a member of the Third Quorum of Seventy and now serves as an Area Seventy in the Europe East Area.

CHAPTER SIXTY-FOUR

Five Hundred Dollars Committed to the Lord

by Francis M. Gibbons

Aside from the sale of onions and radishes to tourists in St. Johns and the sale of magazines and newspapers in Phoenix when I was a boy, my first job was as a bag boy, cashier, and grocery stocker with the A. J. Bayless Markets in Phoenix, Arizona. After the death of my father, Judge A. S. Gibbons, J. B. Bayless told me how I got my first job with Bayless Markets. It was during the mid-thirties in the depths of the depression. One summer my mother, Adeline Christensen Gibbons, complained that my unfilled leisure was a major annoyance to her and pleaded with my father to get me out of her hair. His solution was to consult his client, A. J. Bayless, and to offer to pay my salary if he would give me a job in one of his stores. The deal was struck and I went to work (I believe in the summer of 1935) at Bayless store No. 6 located at Jefferson Street and Seventeenth Avenue in Phoenix near the state capitol building. My beginning salary was 20 cents an hour. Each week during the time he subsidized my employment, my father would go to the store manager, Lee Bowcutt, at the end of the week, find out how many hours I had worked and would give Lee the money which was then passed on to me. This benevolent fraud continued for only several weeks when my father was told that I was doing a good job and that the store would thereafter pay my salary. During my last three years of high school, I worked there at least thirty hours a week, from four to seven Monday through Friday and from six in the morning to midnight Saturday. And each first Sunday, we took inventory, which occupied almost six hours.

My father never told me how I got the job at Bayless. As indicated, I learned about it after his death. I am sure he felt that it would hurt my self-image had I known the circumstances under which I was employed. I have always been grateful for this sensitivity toward my feelings and for the concern he and my mother had for my well-being and success.

From the time I began working there, I regularly saved as much money as I could. It was deposited in a savings account and I took great pride in seeing the balance accumulate through deposits and interest. In those three years, I saved enough to pay entirely for my studies at business college and to provide for my own spending money while I studied since I quit my job during that time. After finishing business college, Bayless hired me to work in the company's office which was then located in back of and above the company's No. 2 store, which was on North Central and Moreland Streets. I worked there from the spring of 1939 until December 1941. During that period, I gave my mother five dollars a week for my room, board and laundry, and after father died in December 1940, I assumed an additional part of the cost of maintaining the family home. I should add that five dollars a week in those days more than covered the family's entire food bill. During this period, I built up my savings account, which had almost been depleted while I was at business college.

Because of the remarkable spiritual experience following my father's death, I had become very active in the Church and had developed a strong desire to fill a mission. In the fall of 1941, I began to look seriously into the possibility of missionary service. I learned that the average monthly cost of a mission in the Southern States at the time was twenty-five dollars, which meant that six hundred dollars would be needed over a two-year period. At the time I had saved five hundred dollars. I wrote to my sister Ruth Gibbons Elliott and asked her if she would lend me a hundred dollars so I could go.

She said she wouldn't lend it to me, but that she would give it to me. And in addition, she bought me a set of matched luggage. (God bless her sweet soul.)

I received my call to the Southern States Mission in November 1941, a month before Pearl Harbor. My group went through the mission home in Salt Lake City in early January 1942, the last large group to be trained until after World War II. The five hundred dollars I committed to the work of the Lord when I entered the mission field was all the earthly wealth I possessed, other than the clothing I took with me and a few pieces of furniture I had purchased, which I left in my mother's home. Although I did not think of it in those terms at the time, it represented an act of total commitment to the work of the Lord and signified my willingness to commit my time, my means, and my talents to building up His kingdom.

Some people who have a restricted view of life and its purpose would consider that I had made a sacrifice. Such as these do not understand that it is not possible to make a sacrifice for the Lord. It was not a sacrifice, but it was one of the greatest blessings ever to come to me and one of the wisest and most profitable investments I ever made. If the reader thinks that I exaggerate, consider these fruits of my spending those five hundred dollars in missionary service:

First, it was the means of bringing the gospel to those whom I taught and baptized, thereby setting them on the road to exaltation, and with whom I expect to have a joyous reunion in the future. Second, I received my personal witness of the Spirit while in the mission field, which has been the keystone to everything I have done since then. Third, it was in the mission field that there was planted in my mind the desire to become an attorney, an honored profession which honed my skills of analysis and expression and which provided the means to raise and educate our children. Fourth, it provided me with my first instruction in the skills of administration and leadership in the church. Fifth, it brought me in contact with two great men, William P. Whitaker and Heber Meeks, whose spiritual sensitivity marked the path of my future. Sixth, it brought me in contact with missionary companions who, over the years, have become choice and much loved friends with whom we have shared the joy of watching our families grow.

Seventh, and most important, it led me to Helen Bay Gibbons, my beloved companion, the mother of our children, who has been and still is a constant source of joy and of motivation. Much of what I have accomplished, small and inconsequential as that might be in the eyes of many, is attributable in no small measure to her love and caring counsel. And, of course, my marriage to Helen has produced our four beloved children; and they and their companions, who are as dear to us as our own children, and their children, our grandchildren, are the very foundation of our eternal inheritance.

If anyone can tell me how to more profitably invest five hundred dollars, I would like to know about it.

CHAPTER SIXTY-FIVE

An Apostle's Promise of Protection

by Francis M. Gibbons

I was called as a bishop in late January 1970 by Russell M. Nelson, who was then the president of the Bonneville Stake. I was sustained in early February at a sacrament meeting in the Yalecrest Ward. Afterward, Elder Richard L. Evans of the Twelve, who was a member of the stake, ordained me and set me apart at a small gathering in the Relief Society room, where all the members of the family were present, including our four children, Suzanne, Mark, Ruth, and Daniel.

Several months later, Mark and Dan drove to Seattle in Mark's VW bug to visit the Elvon Bay family who then lived there. One afternoon, Dan went with David Bay on his paper route, and Mark followed along in the VW. One customer lived in a rear apartment; and when the little boys walked up the driveway to reach it, a snarling dog frightened them, causing them to run away. Daniel, without looking, ran into the street in front of a passing car. Mark, who was sitting in the VW, saw what happened in his rear view mirror. The car, which appeared to be travelling about twenty-five miles an hour, struck Daniel, throwing him up over the hood of the car and on to the road. The thought came to Mark that his brother would either be killed or seriously injured by the impact. He got out of his car and ran fast to Daniel's side. He found his brother sitting in the street, fully conscious, with his head thrust forward to prevent the blood from his nose from getting on his clothing. Daniel's chief concern seemed to be that his new shirt would be soiled with blood. Because of the blood and the force of the impact, it was assumed that Daniel was seriously injured. So, an ambulance was called to take him to the hospital. There, following a complete examination, he was found to be unhurt, except for some bruises and scratches and the fracture of a small bone in his nose. The doctor merely put a small patch over his nose and released him.

The Sunday after the boys returned from Seattle, Daniel attended his deacon's quorum meeting. There his quorum advisor, Max B. Clark, noticing the patch on his nose, asked Daniel if there was anything connected with it that might interest the quorum. In responding, Daniel said in substance, "When Elder Richard L. Evans ordained my father a bishop, he promised that during the period of his service, the members of his family would be specially blessed and protected." Daniel attributed his lack of serious injury to the ordination blessing Elder Evans had given to me.

At the dinner table that Sunday, we asked the children if anything unusual or special had happened at church that morning. Daniel then told of the report he had made to his quorum. As we discussed it, each of the children remembered distinctly the promise Elder Evans had made for their special protection. Significantly, neither Helen nor I remembered this part of the blessing. But in Daniel's case, he not only remembered it, but did so with such a focus of faith that he claimed the blessing.

There is a faith-promoting sequel to this story. Several years later when Daniel had his own VW, he was driving home one night from his job as a janitor at the Church Administration Building. As he travelled east on Second Avenue, a car failed to stop at the B Street intersection. To avoid a collision, Daniel turned the wheel sharply, which caused his car to roll. As it did so, he grasped the wheel tightly with his arms and hands, anchoring it against his body, which prevented him from being thrown out of the car. It came to rest on the lawn of a nearby house. The screeching of tires and the noise caused by the car as it rolled and scraped over the pavement, brought the neighbors running. They managed to pry the door open and to remove Daniel from the car whose roof was mashed almost flat and whose interior was a shambles of torn upholstery and shattered glass. Assuming that Daniel was seriously injured, the neighbors insisted that he lie on the grass under a blanket until the ambulance came. He was conscious throughout the ordeal, though perhaps a little stunned for a while. But as he lay there and took stock of his situation, he found he was not cut, that he was in no great pain, and that there appeared to be no fractures. Realizing this, the thought came to him as he lay there, "Well, even though Dad is no longer the bishop of our ward but is the president of our stake, Elder Evans' blessing is still in effect." So when he had recovered sufficiently from the shock of the accident, he got up, refused to accept any assistance and called a wrecker to move his car up to the Yale Avenue home. He had the driver leave it on Eighteenth East, just east of the house. Not long afterward, Helen returned home from a meeting in the ward to be greeted by the sight of Daniel's demolished car parked on the street. Almost frantic with the thought that her baby had been either killed or seriously injured, she ran into the house calling out to the family to ask what had happened. In answering, Daniel came walking nonchalantly into the hall, in perfect health with no cuts, no fractures and nothing to show for the accident except for some body bruises, which apparently were caused when he cradled himself over the steering wheel.

CHAPTER SIXTY-SIX

A Father's Blessing Fulfilled

by Daniel Bay Gibbons

Before my son Daniel left Salt Lake City to attend law school at Willamette University in 1983, I gave him a father's blessing at his request. In it I promised him, among other things, that he would graduate from law school "with distinction."

Some months after entering law school, the stake president in Salem, Oregon, called Daniel to serve as the elders quorum president in his ward. It was the only time I was tempted to try to intervene in the private life of one of our children after reaching adulthood. I almost called the stake president to point out how difficult law school is, especially during the first year, and that knowing Daniel, as I did, I was sure he would give the church work precedence and that therefore his academic work would suffer. However, on reflection, I refrained from interfering.

Daniel did as I expected. He gave preference to his elders quorum work, which was heavy and continuing since most of the members of the quorum were less active brethren. As a result, his law studies suffered. He did well academically, but not to the level that would have enabled him to compete for spots on law review. Accordingly, when the law review staff for the coming year was appointed at the end of his first year, he didn't make it. Ordinarily this means that a law student will never make law review. However, at the end of his second year in 1985, second-year students were invited to prepare legal articles for consideration by the law review staff and advisors, and those whose papers met certain standards of professionalism would be invited to join the law review staff.

During the summer while Daniel clerked at the Utah Attorney General's Office, he worked on a special paper during his off hours. It was presented to the law review advisors and staff and was judged to be of the high quality necessary to justify his appointment to the Law Review Staff. So during his last year of law school, he was one of the editors of *The Willamette Law Review*, and he graduated with that distinction, a distinction gained by only a select number of law school graduates. Daniel had the faith to claim the priesthood blessing given to him, and the Lord was pleased to reward him for his faith and for his willingness to respond to the call of his priesthood leader.

CHAPTER SIXTY-SEVEN

How a Future Scribe to the Prophets Learned Shorthand

by Daniel Bay Gibbons

My father, Francis M. Gibbons, served as a scribe, confidant and secretary to seven Presidents (or future Presidents) of the Church: Joseph Fielding Smith, Harold B. Lee, Spencer W. Kimball, Ezra Taft Benson, Howard W. Hunter, Gordon B. Hinckley, and Thomas S. Monson. His service in this special capacity began in April of 1970, when he was called as the secretary to the First Presidency.

The calling of secretary to the First Presidency is unique in the Church. Joseph Smith and Brigham Young had a various scribes and secretaries in the early days of the Church, including Oliver Cowdery, Thomas Bullock, William Clayton, George W. Robinson, and many others both official and unofficial. However, the position of secretary to the First Presidency as now constituted was created by President Brigham Young in about 1867 and has been occupied by only five men in the intervening 147 years: George Francis Gibbs (from 1867 to 1923), Joseph W. Anderson (from 1923 to 1970), Francis Marion Gibbons (from 1970 to 1986), Francis Michael Watson (from 1986 to 2008), and Brook P. Hales (from 2008 to the present).

One of the most important functions of the secretary to the First Presidency is to take down minutes of meetings of the First Presidency and Quorum of the Twelve, including the weekly Thursday Council Meetings held in the "Upper Room" on the fourth floor of the Salt Lake Temple. Since recording devices are not used in those meetings, the secretary must take down the verbatim minutes in shorthand.

There is a remarkable sequence of spiritual experiences, which prepared and qualified my father for his special work with the prophets. The first of these was his learning shorthand as a young boy.

Dad grew up in the rural town of St. Johns, Arizona, the youngest child of Andrew Smith Gibbons and Adeline Christensen. Dad's father was a State Superior Court Judge with jurisdiction over the vast Apache County, which included most of northeast Arizona. Judge Gibbons served on the bench until 1930, presiding over a varied trial calendar, hearing both civil and criminal matters. Because the Superior Court was a court of record under the Arizona Constitution, the court employed a full-time court reporter, Ward Heap, who took down a verbatim transcript of all court proceedings.

Dad and his older brother and sisters often visited their father in his courtroom. At the time, Dad would have been less than nine years old. The courtroom and judge's chambers were located on the second story of the courthouse, which was one of the largest buildings in St. Johns. Dad especially loved being in his father's chambers, which were located immediately adjacent to the judge's bench in the courtroom. Dad has commented on his fascination with a rotating bookcase in his father's law library, and with "the peculiar odor that permeated all of the St. Johns courthouse, which was a mixture of stale tobacco smoke, chewing tobacco, and chemicals that were used to clean and sweep the floors." The courtroom itself was a large, impressive room with richly carved wood paneling, a raised bench for the judge, and special built-in desks or enclosures for witnesses, the jury, the clerk and the court reporter. Dad's family has enjoyed telling of the occasion when Dad's sister, Ruth, hid herself under the bench and her father, Judge Gibbons, did not discover her presence until after he had commenced his court session and he felt Ruth tickling his leg.

As for Dad, in visiting his father's courtroom he was most impressed with the transcription work of Ward Heap, the court reporter. This, of course, was before the days of mechanical or electronic recording devices, and court reporters made verbatim transcripts using only a pen, ink and their skill at shorthand. Dad recalled:

> I was enthralled with Ward Heap's reporting. He had an ink well that was affixed to a ring that he put on his left index finger, and then he used a dip pen and would dip into the ink well and write very fast. I was fascinated by that, and that was the thing that motivated me to study shorthand so as to become a court reporter. (Daniel Bay Gibbons with Francis M. Gibbons, October 10, 2001)

So impressed was Dad with the work of his father's court reporter, that he began to aspire to someday be a court reporter himself. This ambition reached fruition a few years later when, at age seventeen, Dad qualified to become a certified court reporter. This occurred while the family was living in Phoenix, Arizona. After working during the summer to save his money, Dad enrolled in the fall of 1938 at the Arizona School of Commerce where he studied shorthand under Kitty Dixon, who had been one of the original pupils of Mr. Gregg, who developed the Gregg shorthand system. In addition to taking a course in shorthand, Dad also took courses in typing, bookkeeping, filing systems, business procedures, and finally an advanced course in shorthand.

Though he qualified as a court reporter in 1938, Dad soon abandoned his ambition to work as a court clerk in the judicial system, and instead turned his attention to business, and later to a full-time mission, service in the U.S. Navy, and then his education at the University of Utah and Stanford University. However, he never lost the ability to write rapidly in shorthand. Indeed, Dad continued to make good use of his shorthand skills throughout his life. For example, during at least two years of his schooling at Stanford University, Dad made all of his diary entries in shorthand.

After serving a full-time mission in the Southern States Mission, Dad was inducted into the Navy during World War II. Because of his ability to take shorthand and to type, he was given an officer's rank upon leaving boot camp, and soon found his way onto the staff of Commodore Brittain, where he had frequent need to use his shorthand. Later Dad took class notes in shorthand in his University and Law School classes, and kept sporadic diary entries in shorthand for many years, including daily entries for the years 1946 through 1948. In his diary entry for Monday, December 6, 1948, Dad wrote:

> I was impressed today to commence keeping my journal in long hand. Perhaps those who might have occasion to read it in years to come will have an easier time reading it.

My mother, Helen Bay Gibbons, was also very skilled in shorthand, and so during the years that their children were growing up, through the 1950's and 1960's they would often communicate with each other in shorthand when they didn't want the children to know the subject of the communication. Thus, during these years it was not uncommon for shorthand messages to appear on the refrigerator or on the desk, written between Dad and Mom in shorthand.

Because recording devices are not used in the meetings of the First Presidency, and especially in the Upper Room of the Temple, the ability to take shorthand rapidly and accurately is one of the most mundane, but at the same time one of the most essential, qualifications for a secretary to the First Presidency. Thus, Dad's early desires to study shorthand and qualify as a certified court reporter are surely providential and crucial in his long preparation to serve with the Presidents of the Church.

CHAPTER SIXTY-EIGHT

"Whether to Make a Lot of Money, or a Great Life"

by Francis M. Gibbons

The account of my call to serve with the First Presidency actually begins in the spring of 1946. I had just been discharged from the United States Navy. Being twenty-five years old and never having had university training, I was concerned about my future and urgently wanted and needed spiritual insight about the path I should follow. Toward this end, I had often engaged in fervent, secret prayer, seeking guidance. At the time we had not been settled long enough in our new location to have received assignments so that we had no responsibilities to make it necessary to attend church in our own ward. One Sunday morning as I read the paper, I noticed that Elder Albert E. Bowen of the Twelve was presiding at a stake conference in the Assembly Hall on Temple Square. Since he was a special favorite of mine because of his superb command of the English language, I wanted to go hear him. Helen agreed, so we rode to Temple Square on the bus from our apartment at 666 Second Avenue. Before going there, I prayed secretly that the Lord, through the Apostle, would reveal something that would be helpful and meaningful in my future life. I did not divulge to Helen the substance of my secret prayers. When we arrived at the Assembly Hall, we took seats near the front on the main floor beneath the south balcony so that we were to the speaker's right as he stood at the pulpit. As I sat in the meeting, I repeated my secret prayers for some spiritual enlightenment about the future. During the course of Elder Bowen's talk, he paused, looked over to his right in our direction and then made this statement which seemed to have no relationship or relevance to anything he had said before: "There often comes a time in a man's life," he said, "when he must decide whether to make a lot of money or a great life." With that, I received a powerful witness of the Spirit, accompanied by a burning in the bosom, that this was the spiritual direction that I sought. As we returned home after the meeting, Helen said to me in substance, "You know Frank, I could not escape the feeling that at one point in his sermon, Elder Bowen was talking directly to you." It was then that I told her for the first time of my strugglings in secret prayer.

After this incident, I completed my studies at Stanford University and the University of Utah, was admitted to the bar and commenced to practice law with Senior & Senior. After several years of practice, I received a telephone call one day from Vernon Snyder, who was then the general counsel for the Church. He asked to meet with me. At the time he offered me a position on his legal staff. The reason for offering a position to me was my familiarity with real estate and real estate transactions. I put him off, saying I wanted to think about it. From the standpoint of my professional status and work, the job had no interest for me. But because of the source of the offer and the spiritual experience I had had with Elder Bowen, I wasn't sure whether I had reached the point where I was faced with a decision whether to make a lot of money or a great life. I was not making a lot of money then, although I was doing well for a young attorney and had high hopes for the future. As I appraised the offer and its implications, I sought the counsel of my friend, Albert R. Bowen, the son of the Apostle, Albert E. Bowen, who had passed away in the meantime. Albert was a prominent attorney in Salt Lake who lived in the Yalecrest Ward of the Bonneville Stake. I learned when I went to confer with him that he had once served as the general counsel for the Church and, therefore, he was in an excellent position to give me good counsel. I told him of the experience I had in the Assembly Hall several years before involving his father and of the dilemma I then faced because of the offer of employment from Vernon Snyder. He gave me good insight into what I might expect if I were to go to work in the Church legal department. He told me that when the job of general counsel was offered to him, he was excited and flattered and went to his father for counsel. The father told him in effect, "Albert, if you go there, there will be twenty-six telephone lines leading to your desk, and you will be on the run all the time." Albert said that notwithstanding that counsel, he took the job but didn't stay very long and soon returned to private practice. After hearing that and after praying about it, I said essentially this to Vernon Snyder: "Vernon, if this is a call from the Brethren, I will join you as soon as I can terminate my relationship with my firm. But if this is merely the offer of a job, I will decline with thanks." When Vernon said it was merely a job offer, I turned it down with good feeling. A few years later, Vernon Snyder came to me again with the same offer. This time, it was easy. I simply asked if it were a call or a job offer. When he said it was a job offer and nothing more, I turned him down again with good feeling and continued with my private practice, until April 1970.

At that time, I was serving as the bishop of the Yalecrest Ward in the Bonneville Stake. In that capacity, I attended the Solemn Assembly on Monday, April 6, 1970, where President Joseph Fielding Smith was sustained as the new Prophet, Seer and Revelator. At the same time, Elder Boyd K. Packer was sustained as the new member of the Twelve to fill the vacancy created by the call of President Harold B. Lee to the First Presidency; and Elders Joseph Anderson, David B. Haight, and William H. Bennett were called as Assistants to the Twelve. At the time, Elder Anderson resided in the Yalecrest Ward where I served as bishop. I had previously served with him for six years on the Bonneville Stake high council, and therefore we were very close. On this account, I said to Helen that evening, "Let's go over and congratulate Joseph and Norma on the call which has come to Joseph." We went to the confectionery, where we bought a box of candy, and went to the Anderson's Yalecrest Avenue home to share the great honor that had come to them that day. We spent about an hour there, during which time Joseph told us of the great difficulty the Brethren were having in finding a replacement for him as the secretary to the First Presidency. Among other things, the man had to be mature and experienced enough to work directly with the General Authorities, should have had substantial administrative experience in the Church, and should be able to take shorthand very rapidly. This last qualification, though relatively unimportant, was essential because the Brethren do not use recording devices in meetings of the First Presidency or in the upper room of the temple and therefore the proceedings at these meetings have to be recorded verbatim and then reduced to concise minutes. As a teenager I had learned shorthand from Kitty Dixon, one of Gregg's original students and had acquired enough speed and accuracy to qualify as a court reporter. In many ways, this sounded like a job description that I could satisfy, and during the conversation the thought crossed my mind that it was a job I could fill. When we got home, Helen said to me in substance, "Frank, I could hardly restrain myself from saying to Brother Anderson, 'The man the brethren are looking for is Frank Gibbons.'" We prayed about it that night and feeling a warm, confirming feeling, we decided that I would inform Brother Anderson of my background and our feelings. I called him the next morning about 7:00 a.m. and asked if I could come to see him. He told me to come at 10:00 a.m. following his Tuesday meeting with the First Presidency. He told me later that after my call, he turned to his wife, Norma, and said "Frank is going to come in and offer his services to the Brethren, to which Norma answered in effect, "You must be wrong; Frank wouldn't give up his legal practice for that." Joseph's only response was, "We'll see."

When I went to see Elder Anderson that morning, Tuesday, April 7, 1970, I merely told him of my background and the impression Helen and I had had and that I merely wanted to say that if the Brethren had need of my services, I was available. He said, "Would you come for ____ dollars?" which was roughly 25% of what I had earned the previous year. When I answered that money was no object, he said something which I cherish and which has been very meaningful to me. He said simply, "Frank, I'm proud of you." He then told me that he would be in touch with me later.

The next day, Wednesday, April 8, Joseph called me and said that the First Presidency wanted to see me at 8:00 a.m. the next morning. When I learned this, I had a great feeling that I wanted to be alone. So, I told my secretary that I wouldn't be back the rest of the day, got in my car, and drove across the valley to the Bingham Mine. There I prayed and reflected for an hour or more and then drove back to the city. As I neared West Jordan, the voice spoke to me and said, "The time is now."

The next morning I met with the First Presidency and Brother Anderson at 8:00 a.m. I had met President Lee over twenty years before when I was a student at Stanford. But I had never formally met President Smith or President Tanner. As we began to talk, it became apparent that I was to be the new secretary to the First Presidency, although that was never expressly stated. I was asked how long it would take to sever the connections with my firm. I answered that it would take several months, although I would be able to commence to do some work with the Brethren immediately. They encouraged me to take as much time as necessary so my firm would not suffer.

President Tanner then said: The only question I have is how can you afford to do it?" to which President Lee responded, "Frank has come to the point in life when he can't afford not to do it." There was no discussion at the time about my compensation or my title or the division of responsibilities with Brother Anderson.

It came out during the conversation that the week before the Brethren almost made a decision about a replacement for Elder Anderson. They had interviewed several men and had one of them, at least, attend a meeting of the First Presidency to try him out. At the time, however, President Lee had said, "Let's wait until after conference to make a decision." At that, President Tanner patted President Lee on the leg and said, "Sometimes you have the inspiration, don't you?"

After a fifteen-minute discussion, the Brethren turned to their regular agenda, which was heavily crowded, as they had to prepare for the council meeting to follow where the new general authorities would be instructed, set apart and, in the case of Elder Boyd Packer, ordained. Elder Anderson handed me a shorthand notebook, and I was at work. About ten minutes to ten, the First Presidency meeting adjourned to go to the temple for the weekly council meeting. No one expressly said I was to go with them. But everyone acted as if it were assumed I would go. Acting on that, I hurriedly called my secretary to say I would not be in the office that day. As we walked to the temple I remember thinking to myself, "Do I have my temple recommend with me? Is it current?" But, no one asked me for it. We walked through the tunnel under Main Street to the temple, took the elevator to the fourth floor and entered the Upper Council Room where the Twelve had been in session since 8:00 a.m. As we entered, the Twelve stood as the First Presidency, Joseph Anderson and I walked around the circle to shake hands with the brethren, including one current and six future Presidents of the Church! In the circle standing in the order of their seniority were Elders Spencer W. Kimball, Ezra Taft Benson, Mark E. Petersen, Delbert L. Stapley, Marion G. Romney, LeGrand Richards, Richard L. Evans, Hugh B. Brown, Howard W. Hunter, Gordon B. Hinckley, Thomas S. Monson and Boyd K. Packer. I knew Elder Stapley quite well, as he was serving as a counselor in the Phoenix Stake Presidency in January 1942 when I left on my mission. Also, he had advanced a hundred dollars to help me complete my mission when it was thought I would be permitted to stay in the field for an additional six months. When I returned to Phoenix in February 1944, I went to his office to return the amount I had not spent. (He sent the money to me when Oscar A. Kirkham called to tell him that I needed money after Elder Kirkham had completed his tour of the mission.) I knew Elder Evans personally from my years of service as a guide on Temple Square when he served as the president of the Square. Also, Elder Evans had ordained me a bishop and had set me apart as the bishop of the Yalecrest Ward only two months before. I also had a nodding acquaintance with Elder Petersen and Elder Brown, who were members of the Bonneville Stake. The others I had never met before. As I shook hands with Elder Stapley he said, "Frank, I didn't know about this until last night." From this it became apparent that the Brethren had checked me out and had made a decision that I was to replace Joseph Anderson before I met with them Thursday morning.

At this meeting, Elder Packer was ordained an Apostle and Elders Anderson, David B. Haight and William H. Bennett were set apart as Assistants to the Twelve. Because Joseph was involved in these ceremonies, the responsibility of keeping the minutes of the meeting fell entirely upon me. The only things we keep a verbatim record of in the meetings of the First Presidency and in the temple are blessings of ordination and setting apart and special statements or instructions of the prophet. All else is later condensed into minutes, although the verbatim notebooks are saved for possible future reference. So at this meeting, I took in shorthand and later had transcribed the ordination of Elder Packer and the settings apart of the three new Assistants. Although it had been thirty-one years since I completed my studies at business college, and although I had not used my shorthand in the interim except to take notes at the university or as I practiced law in court, I don't think I missed a single word. This has always seemed a little miraculous to me and has suggested to my mind that because of the extraordinary way in which I had found my way to the upper room of the temple that the Lord had a hand in preparing me and leading me along, for which I was and am grateful to Him.

So within three days after attending the solemn assembly on April 6, 1970, I found myself suddenly and unexpectedly set upon a new career path. At the time I had been practicing law for eighteen years, was a full partner in a prestigious law firm with a personal A-V rating from my peers, owned my own home free and clear, was debt free, and had comfortable surpluses. Because of my training, legal status, and associations, I have no doubt that had I remained in the practice of law, in a few years afterward I would have made a lot of money in a profession which I loved. As I have reflected about these extraordinary circumstances, I have seriously questioned whether I would have had the courage and faith to turn my back on all this had not the Lord planted in my mind the prophetic statement made by Elder Albert E. Bowen twenty-four years before. I thank the Lord for that spiritual guidance.

There are three other aspects about this experience which are significant. First, despite the drastic reduction in my income, we lived as well after my call as before it. We later made substantial contributions to the children for their missions, education and in helping them to become settled in their own homes. Yet now many years later, we have a substantial "nest egg" which, with retirement, social security and income from book royalties, will enable us to live comfortably without concern about finances. Again, the Lord has blessed us in a miraculous way. Second, during all the years I practiced law, and before, I had the goal of being able to retire by age 55 and to spend the rest of my days writing Church history. The way things worked out, my prayers were answered six years in advance, because at age 49 I began to write the ongoing history of the First Presidency through the minutes I kept and my personal diaries. In addition, the inspired incentive I received to write biographies of all the presidents of the Church has led me into a rich field of historical research and writing I never dreamed of. And third, late in 1969, just a few months before I became the secretary to the First Presidency, I began to keep indexes of my diaries, something I had never done during the previous twenty-seven years of diary keeping. As a result, for the entire period of my service with the First Presidency, and since then, I have completely indexed diaries, indexed by name, place and subject matter.

In these things, I see again the hand of the Lord, leading me along, whispering to me, inspiring me, and helping me to perform and to become prepared to perform the things that I have been sent here to do.

CHAPTER SIXTY-NINE

A Liahona
at the Door of My Tent
by Daniel Bay Gibbons

I love the account of the finding of the Liahona in 1 Nephi 16. It simply appeared, lying "upon the ground" at the door of Lehi's tent one morning. The account speaks of the "astonishment" everyone experienced at the appearance of this mysterious thing. It was described as "a round ball of curious workmanship." Lehi and his family quickly discovered some of the properties of this "ball." For example, they saw that there were two spindles inside the ball, and they figured out that "the one pointed the way whither we should go into the wilderness." (1 Nephi 16:10)

There is no mention of the use of the second spindle, and I think this is instructive. At first Lehi didn't know everything about the ball or its meaning. I would like to compare the ball, or as the descendants of Lehi later called it, the Liahona, to spiritual experiences which we have in our lives. These spiritual experiences come unannounced. They simply appear at the door of our tent. We are often astonished by these experiences. We discern some meaning in them. We figure out what one of the spindles can do. Then, like Lehi, we pursue our journeys and think we have it all figured out. The spiritual experience has come. We make use of it. We think we have exhausted its meaning. And then we forget it.

Some of the Liahonas that appear at the doors of our tents are impressions we have about the future. Some of them are miracles that occur, such as healings. Some of them are priesthood blessings received, such as patriarchal blessings. Some of them are prophetic utterances spoken by us or to us. Some of them are dreams, or visions, or even the ministering of angels. We receive the spiritual experience. We ponder it. We derive guidance or blessing or uplift from it. And then we move on and we forget the experience.

I want to tell you about a Liahona which appeared at the door of my tent one morning. In the early morning hours of October 3, 2001, I awoke from a very vivid and powerful dream. Here is my diary entry from that morning:

> I just awoke with the most vivid and powerful dream. It seemed that I was traveling with Julie in a most beautiful area of pine trees and birch trees in Eastern Europe or Russia. We stopped at a large church building. My eyes were filled with tears as Julie and I walked through the building, which seemed to be empty. We found that we were in a large building with a large chapel, offices, and classrooms. We wandered around. In the chapel we heard the voice of one of the brethren—I think it was Elder Russell M. Nelson—almost as if General Conference were being broadcast to an empty chapel. Then a woman walked toward us from some other part of the building. She was a simple and plain woman with a kindly and strong face—an older Latter-day Saint woman—who hugged Julie and then began talking with Julie as best as she could in Russian, almost as if she was making us at home. She greeted me and hugged me, and I remember in the brief embrace that she smelled so sweet. This woman then took Julie down the hall to a kitchen, chattering as she went. I was then led into an adjoining room by two men. There were piles of maps—large detailed maps—on a table, and we started going over these and talking about the far-flung branches of the Church in the forests, including branches in Russia. We also talked about the need to travel to these different places. He said that they were looking for a man who spoke these languages, including Russian. The man told me, in English, that they needed not only

someone with language skills, but someone of substance in the Church who could "be a shepherd and direct and lead the far-flung branches to the North and East." There was then a phone call for me. On the phone was a woman from the Church's Area Office. She asked me if I understood the significance of what the man was telling me.

I then almost immediately awoke with the most powerful warm and peaceful feeling, and with the strong impression that the time may come when I may serve the Church in some far-flung part of the globe. I was filled with a powerful, humble, warm spirit, and with the commitment that I would give up everything I have—everything I am, everything I possess— to serve the Lord with my family. I knelt down by my bed and rededicated myself to the Lord's service, then came downstairs immediately to my study to write out the dream. (Daniel Bay Gibbons Diary, October 3, 2001)

So this was the "Liahona" which appeared to my great astonishment one morning.

Naturally I pondered this dream. I thought about it. I studied it. I even shared it with my wife and children, Annie, Jenny, Liz, Abby, and Josh. And I obtained some direction from it. For example, from the time of this dream I commenced once more, after a break of almost a quarter of a century, in studying the Russian language. I recalled that in 1976, I had a special experience while serving in Germany and had the impression that I ought to learn Russian and had actually taken Russian at the University of Utah from 1978 to 1979. So after receiving this dream in October of 2001, I bought a Russian edition of *The Book of Mormon* and started to read it, beginning with 1 Nephi 1:1, where I read, "Я Нефий," ("I Nephi") in Russian. I remembered that "Я" meant "I," and I figured out that "Нефий" meant "Nephi," but from that point forward I was looking up words constantly from my dictionary. But every day I read a little in the Russian *Book of Mormon*, and after about two and half years, I finished it. I then began it again and read it a second time. Then a third time. I was pursuing my journey, like Lehi, having taken my bearings from one spindle in my little Liahona.

After discovering the Liahona, Lehi and his family set out immediately and pursued their journey. We read in 1 Nephi 16 that the spindle sent them in a south-southeast direction for several days and they made a new camp. Then Nephi and his brothers took their bows and went out to find food. Here is when the crisis struck. Nephi broke his bow, which was made of steel. The universal reaction of Nephi's brothers and even his father was despair and sorrow. But Nephi found a piece of wood, and a straight stick and stones, and made new weapons. He did the best he could. Then, interestingly, he went to his father to ask where he should go to find food. Lehi humbled himself and prayed, and the answer he obtained is astonishing!

> And it came to pass that the voice of the Lord said unto him: Look upon the ball, and behold the things which are written. And it came to pass that when my father beheld the things which were written upon the ball, he did fear and tremble exceedingly, and also my brethren and the sons of Ishmael and our wives. And it came to pass that I, Nephi, beheld the pointers which were in the ball, that they did work according to the faith and diligence and heed which we did give unto them. And there was a new writing, which was plain to be read, which did give us understanding concerning the ways of the Lord; and it was written and changed from time to time, according to the faith and diligence which we gave unto it. And thus we see that by small means the Lord can bring about great things. (1 Nephi 16:26-29)

The lesson is that the Liahonas that may appear at the doors of our tents may have far more significance in our lives than we at first discern. Spiritual experiences that we have can yield new insights over time. It is almost as if there is new meaning "written" upon our spiritual experiences, which we at first do not or cannot notice. Only through time and experience and continued searching will our Liahonas reveal their marvelous mysteries and unfold new blessings. This is often true with patriarchal blessings, which over a period of years and decades acquire significance and meaning far beyond the comprehension of a young teenage recipient to appreciate.

The "Liahona" of my dream had given me a direction, to once more pick up my study of Russian. Then, more than three years later, Julie and I discovered "a new writing, which was plain to be read, which did give us understanding concerning the ways of the Lord." Julie had a dream, which I recorded in my diary on March 3, 2005, as follows:

> Julie recently related to me a vivid dream that she had. She said that she and I were together teaching in a large room filled with Chinese young people.

Like my dream, Julie and I knew that this dream was significant. We both felt the Spirit strongly testify that the dream had spiritual significance. Like the first dream, we pondered it and wondered what it meant. At that point, the only direction we could glean from it was that it seemed to hint that we would be teaching together, as if on a mission. We started to talk more about the possibility of serving a mission together. We started to study more. It was about this time that I bought us copies of *Preach My Gospel*, and our scripture study improved. And like Lehi, we continued our journey, having some direction, but not really knowing how it would all turn out.

Then, in 2010 I received a very surprising phone call one day. I was at work in my courthouse, presiding over a jury trial. I had taken a recess and returned to my chambers when the phone rang. It was Elder Dallin H. Oaks of the Quorum of the Twelve on the line. Though I had never met him, I instantly recognized his voice. He asked me if Julie and I could come to his office to spend an hour with him. Two days later we found ourselves in the Church Administration Building in Elder Oaks' office. He told us that it was an "exploratory" interview to consider the possibility of our receiving a call to preside over one of the missions of the Church. We had a nice visit and left with the instruction that we were not to discuss the interview with anyone, even our children, and that if a mission call were extended, we would be contacted by the First Presidency between November 15 and December 15.

For the next two months we were in a state of great uncertainty. We knew that a mission call was a possibility. Elder Oaks had also commented on my Russian language background and said that if a call were extended, it *might* be to a Russian-speaking mission. We learned that Russian-speaking missions in the Baltic States, in Kyiv and Donetsk, Ukraine, and in St. Petersburg, Yekaterinburg, and Novosibirsk Russia would be receiving new mission presidents in 2011, but it was still speculative as to whether we would even be called, let alone to a Russian mission.

In this time of uncertainty, Julie and I went often to the temple to ponder and pray. In November of 2010 we were together in the Salt Lake Temple, when we received additional insight about the dreams we had received in 2001 and 2005. During the endowment session, as is our tradition, we stood together in one of the rooms to pray. During the prayer, spoken by one of the ordinance workers in the temple, he made the request "that the doors of nations not open to the preaching of the gospel will be fully opened." When he said this, it was if an electric shock went through my body. I felt the Spirit strongly, and I knew that Julie had the same experience, because she squeezed my hand during the prayer.

Afterwards we sat in the celestial room of the temple talking quietly to each other. We commented on the feeling we had both had during the prayer, and wondered what it meant.

Julie said, "Remember the dream I had about teaching Chinese young people? Maybe we will receive a call to go to China!"

"That doesn't make sense," I said. "In my dream, we were in Russia. And besides, China is not yet fully opened to missionary work."

We sat and pondered. Then I made a comment, which in retrospect, was inspired. "Maybe it wasn't China," I said. "Maybe it was Mongolia. Remember, Novosibirsk is close to Mongolia."

So, time went on, and in a few weeks we received a phone call from President Henry B. Eyring's secretary, and soon found ourselves in his office for an inspiring hour. He extended a call for us to preside over an English-speaking mission! We accepted the call, but couldn't help but wonder about the "English-speaking" assignment. What about the impression I had had in Germany in 1976? What about my dream of 2001? What about Julie's dream of the "Chinese young people?" Like Nephi we did the best we could and followed the direction of the Lord and His servants and accepted the call. I resigned my judgeship, we set our affairs in order to the best of our ability, and we prepared to serve an English-speaking mission. In February of 2011 we were assigned to the Arkansas Little Rock Mission. We corresponded with the incumbent president, memorized the names of all the missionaries, and prepared to serve in Arkansas, Tennessee, and Mississippi. I bought several books about the history of the region, and as the date approached, we felt ready to serve in the South.

Then, in mid-June of 2011, there was another "new writing" upon our Liahona. Elder Richard G. Hinckley of the Seventy called one afternoon to read me a letter from the First Presidency. They were "pleased," it read, to announce to us that our mission assignment had been changed to the Russia Novosibirsk Mission.

There followed a frantic time in our lives. We applied for Russian visas, and I again took up my Russian studies in earnest. We knew that after the mission presidents' seminar in June, we would need to wait another month for our Russian visas, and so made arrangements to live and study in the MTC. We ultimately arrived in Russia the first week of August 2011.

But first, we had additional "writings" upon our Liahona. In late June we were set apart for our missions in the office of Elder Russell M. Nelson of the Quorum of the Twelve. On the morning of our setting apart, we awoke, and the first thing Julie said to me was, "What does 'Krasnoyarsk' mean?"

"'Krasnoyarsk' is the name of a city in our mission," I told her.

"Oh," she said. "That's funny. I've had it going through my head all night: 'Krasnoyarsk! Krasnoyarsk! Krasnoyarsk!'"

"That's strange," I said, but we both sensed that there was significance in this.

A few hours later we were in Elder Nelson's office with our Utah-based children and my parents. Elder Nelson came in the room with Elder Ronald A. Rasband of the Presidency of the Seventy. Elder Rasband was to set Julie apart. Elder Rasband commented on the last-minute change in our mission assignment from Arkansas to Russia, and then said, "The Lord knew all along where He wanted you to serve. It just took us a little while to figure it out."

Before setting me apart as a mission president, Elder Nelson said to us, "Before giving Daniel his blessing, I would like to tell you about an experience I had in your mission several years ago, in the city of Krasnoyarsk." Julie and I looked at each other, sensing that here was something else of significance in our unfolding understanding of "the ways of the Lord." "I attended a youth conference in Krasnoyarsk," Elder Nelson continued, "and when I looked into the faces of the young people there, I had a witness that the blood of Israel was very strong in their veins, and that they and their ancestors had been brought to that place to be prepared for the preaching of the Gospel and to be preserved from the blood and sins of their generation."

Following our setting apart, Julie and I had dinner at the Lion House with our children Annie, Liz, Abby, and Josh, as well as with Abby's husband, Ryan. During dinner Abby said, "Dad. Do you remember that dream you had years ago? When we get home, will you read it to us again?" And so that evening I pulled out my diary and read the account of the dream I had received in October of 2001, ten years before, and we marveled at how the Lord had prepared us and over a decade had continued to unfold for us His purposes, and give us new insights about the "Liahona" which had appeared so astonishingly at the door of our tent.

There are two sequels to this long story of our personal "Liahona," which led us to serve on the other side of the world. First, a few weeks after arriving in Russia, the General Authorities first discussed with me the possibility of Kazakhstan becoming part of our mission, and in May of 2012, Julie and I made our first trip there. When we sat in sacrament meeting in the beautiful large hall where the saints meet in Almaty, and looked at the distinctively Asian faces of most of the members, Julie and I looked at each other with tears in our eyes. We now had a greater understanding of her dream. They weren't Chinese young people, or Mongolian. They were Kazakhs! And we had a sense that we were in the right place at the right time.

Finally, we had a most inspiring confirmation of the Lord's guidance of our journey when we first traveled to Krasnoyarsk in August of 2011, but this confirmation was preceded by a crisis, a "broken bow" moment. A few days after we arrived in Russia I received a telephone call from our young district president in Krasnoyarsk, Denis Nozhnikov. Denis was a returned missionary with a beautiful young family and was reported to me as being one of the finest young leaders in Russia. President Nozhnikov told me that he faced an unexpected challenge in his business, and would either need to close his business in Russia, or move it entirely to Ukraine. "What shall I do, President?" he asked. I told him that I couldn't tell him what to do, but that the Lord would tell him. We then discussed the Lord's process of decision making outlined in the *Doctrine and Covenants*, Sections 8 and 9: that is, we first study things out in our mind, then consult our hearts, and finally we pray about them. A few days later Denis called me and told me that he felt certain the Lord wanted him to return to Ukraine.

This posed a great dilemma for me, as the departure of one of our strongest leaders greatly weakened our Church organization in Siberia. At the time we had fourteen small branches spread out over a thousand miles in three small member districts, none of which were fully organized or fully functioning. To lose a great leader was a great blow to the work. I felt like Nephi, whose bow of fine steel was broken.

I also felt personally inadequate. All of the mission presidents I had ever known were men of maturity and experience and usually of great temporal success. Most of them were fully retired from successful careers. Most of them had served in stake presidencies. I was a young man who had never been in a stake presidency and was far from retirement. I felt like I personally knew hundreds of men in the Church who would make better mission presidents than I possibly could. I approached the Lord in prayer, asking for guidance and help.

So, with heavy hearts, Julie and I made our first trip to Krasnoyarsk in August of 2011. We traveled by overnight train, a trip of about fourteen hours. The summer months have long days, with late sunsets and early sunrises, and through the night I could not sleep, but sat by the window in our private compartment watching the beautiful landscape of pine trees and birch trees. As we traveled, I was praying fervently for help from the Lord.

Then, as we reached the outskirts of Krasnoyarsk, I had one of the most profound spiritual experiences of my mission. I formulated in my mind what the missionaries would call "an inspired question." It was this: "Would it be possible to combine all of our Russian branches and member districts into one large district, which in time could become a stake?" The Spirit manifested to me that the answer was yes! And in that moment, I knew the chief thrust of my three-year assignment in Siberia: to establish centers of strength that could become a stake in the foreseeable future!

As we entered Krasnoyarsk and rode through its streets by taxi that morning, I was filled with gratitude for the inspiration that had turned a "broken bow" into a new and powerful instrument. I now knew my course—one dictated by the Lord.

A few hours later we drove to the beautiful branch building in Krasnoyarsk to meet with the missionaries. We arrived on a beautiful Saturday morning. There was a widow member tending flowers in the Church yard beside the lovely white walls. Then, as we entered the building itself, it struck me! This was the building of my dream! In every detail, this was the building I had dreamed about in 2001! It was the same chapel, the same hallways, the same kitchen, the same office! This was the final unfolding of the dream of the night I had received ten years earlier! In that moment, I felt profound peace and gratitude! I knew the Lord was at the helm, giving us "Liahonas" to guide our paths, helping us make course corrections, getting us where we need to be to do what He wants us to do.

And in that moment, I also had this testimony: I may not be the best mission president, but I'm the right one! I'm the right one! And that's all that matters.

I testify that the Lord places "Liahonas" from time to time by the doors to our tents, and that over time he gives us additional understanding about their use and meaning. God lives. This is His work. Of this I testify, in the name of Jesus Christ, Amen!

Daniel Bay Gibbons

Holladay, Utah

July 31, 2014

Select Bibliography

Anderson, Joseph, *Prophets I Have Known*, (Salt Lake City: Deseret Book, 1973)

Ballard, Margaret McNeil, "My Story," in *Our Pioneer Heritage*, comp. Kate B. Carter, 20 vols. (Salt Lake City: Daughters of the Utah Pioneers, 1959-77), 3:199-206.

Bassett, Theda Lucille. *Grandpa Neibaur was a Pioneer*. (Salt Lake City: Artistic Printing Co., 1988)

Black, Susan Easton. *Membership of The Church of Jesus Christ of Latter-day Saints: 1830-1848*. 49 volumes. Published by The Corporation of the President of The Church of Jesus Christ of Latter-day Saints, Salt Lake City, Utah, (1990)

Brassanini, Pedro and Betty Brassanini, Interview of Pedro and Betty Brassanini conducted by Francis M. Gibbons.

Britsch, R. Lanier, "The Latter Day Saint Mission to India, 1851–1856", *BYU Studies*, Vol. 12 No. 3, (Spring 1972), p. 262.

Brown, Lois Decker, "Brief Mission, Constant Harvest," *Ensign*, August 1995

Carter, Kate B. *Treasures of Pioneer History*. Salt Lake City: Daughters of Utah Pioneers, (1952), 1:333-40.

Corbett, Don C., *Mary Fielding Smith: Daughter of Britain,* Salt Lake City: Deseret Book Co., (1966).

Cowan, Richard O., "Mischa Markow: Mormon Missionary to the Balkans", in *Brigham Young University Studies*. 33 vols. Provo, Utah: Brigham Young University Press, 1959-1996, Autumn 1970, pg. 92.

Cowley, Matthew, *Matthew Cowley Speaks*. (Salt Lake City: Deseret Book 1954).

Cowley, Matthias Foss, *Wilford Woodruff, His Life and Labors* (Salt Lake City: Bookcraft 1964).

Gibbons, Andrew Smith, Diaries of Andrew Smith Gibbons, Church Historical Department

Gibbons, Francis M., *David O. McKay: Apostle to the World, Prophet of God:* Deseret Book, Salt Lake City (1986).

Gibbons, Francis M., *George Albert Smith: Kind and Caring Christian, Prophet of God*, (Salt Lake City: Deseret Book 1990)

Gibbons, Francis M., *Heber J. Grant: Man of Steel, Prophet of God*, pp.12–13, 34–35, Deseret Book (1979).

Gibbons, Francis M., *Wilford Woodruff, Wondrous Worker, Prophet of God*, Deseret Book Company (1987)

Gibbons, Daniel Bay, Missionary Diaries 1976-1978 and 2011-2014

Gibbons, Francis M., "Biography of Andrew Smith Gibbons," in Gibbons, Francis M. and Helen Bay Gibbons, *Nana and the Judge*, privately published, (Salt Lake City, 1978)

Gibbons, Francis M., Interviews conducted by Daniel Bay Gibbons, 2001 to 2014

Gibbons, Francis M., Missionary Diaries 1942-1944

Gibbons, Francis M., *My Spiritual Testament*, (Salt Lake City: privately published, 1989)

Gibbons, Francis M. and Daniel Bay Gibbons, A Gathering of Eagles (New York: iUniverse, 2002)

Gibbons, Helen B., "Life sketch of Pedro Brassanini", unpublished manuscript

Gibbons, Helen Bay, "Life Sketch of Roberta MacKnight Hunt", based on personal interviews conducted by Helen Bay Gibbons.

Gibbons, Helen Bay, *Saint and Savage*, (Salt Lake City: Deseret Book, 1965)

Gibbons, Richard, Unpublished biography of Andrew Smith Gibbons by his son, Richard Gibbons

Grover, Mark L., "The Mormon Priesthood Revelation and the Sao Paulo Brazil Temple", in *Dialogue*, Vol. 23, No. 1, Spring 1990, Page 39.

Guschin, Yuri, "Прояблять веру и роботать вместе ц миссионерами," Liahona (Russian Edition), December 2013, pages H1-H2.

"Hopi Hearings" conducted July 15–30, 1955, Phoenix Office, Hopi Agency, conducted by a team appointed by Mr. Glenn L. Emmons, Commissioner of Indian Affairs, and composed of Thomas W. Reid, Joe Jennings and Graham Holmes.

Jenson, Andrew, *Encyclopedic History of The Church of Jesus Christ of Latter-day Saints,*)Salt Lake City: Deseret News Publishing Company 1941)

Jenson, Andrew. *Latter-day Saint Biographical Encyclopedia: A Compilation of Biographical Sketches of Prominent Men and Women in the Church of Jesus Christ of Latter-day Saints.* 4 vols. (Salt Lake City: A. Jenson History Company)

Johnson, Joseph William Billy. "We Felt the Spirit of the Pioneers." *In* LeBaron, E. Dale. *All Are Alike unto God.* Salt Lake City (1990), pp. 13 – 23.

Journal History of the East India Mission, Branch Record, p. 1. Friday, 26 December 1851 (record kept by the LDS Church Historian's Office, Salt Lake City, Utah).

Lythgoe, Dennis, *Education Pioneer,* (Salt Lake City: Deseret News, June 26, 1998), page C–1.

Ludlow, Daniel H., ed., "Oceania, the Church In," in *Encyclopedia of Mormonism,* Vol.3.

Markow, Mischa, "Life and History," LDS Church Archives, (n.p., n.d.).

Martins, Helvecio and Ruta Martins, Interview of Helvecio Martins and Ruta Martins, conducted in Sao Paulo Brazil by Helen Bay Gibbons.

McAllister, Jack, "The Unlikely Daniel Webster Jones: First Spanish Translations from the Book of Mormon", *Ensign* (August 1981) pages 50 – 52.

McClintock, James H.: *Mormon Settlements in Arizona,* (Phoenix 1921)

McKay, Llewelyn, R., *Home Memories of President David O. McKay,* Deseret Book, Salt Lake City (1956).

Millennial Star, August 19, 1915, volume 77, pages 523 to 524.

Miner, Caroline Eyring, History of Miles Romney and Elizabeth Gaskell Romney, Publishers Press (1978).

Neibaur, Alexander. "Autobiography, LDS Church Archives" *in* Backman, Milton V. Jr., and Keith W. Perkins, ed. *Writings of Early Latter-day Saints and Their Contemporaries, A Database Collection.* Excerpts. 2nd ed., rev. and enlarged. (Provo, Utah: Religious Studies Center, 1996).

Nelson, Russell M., "Drama on the European Stage", *Ensign*, (December 1991), pages 7 through 17. (Page 12).

Numkena, Wil, Transcript of Interview of Wil Numkena, Director of the Utah State Division of Indian Affairs and a great grandson of Tuba, conducted by Helen Bay Gibbons December 15, 1992

Obinna, Anthony Uzodimma. "Voice from Nigeria." *Ensign* 10 (December 1980): 28-30.

Ogden, D. Kelly, "Two from Judah Ministering to Joseph" *in* Garrett, H. Dean., ed. *Regional Studies in Latter-day Saint History: Illinois.* Provo: Department of Church History and Doctrine (1995).

Ott, C. Eric, "In the Lord's Time," *Ensign*, May 1989.

Palmer, Spencer J., *The Church Encounters Asia.* Salt Lake City, Utah: Deseret Book Company, (1970).

Richardson, Arthur, *The Life and Ministry of John Morgan*, Nicholas G. Morgan, Sr. (Salt Lake City: 1965).

Rivers, Percy John, *Autobiography of Percy John Rivers*, Edited by Jennie Hart (1992)

Roberts, Brigham H., *A Comprehensive History of the Church of Jesus Christ of Latter-day Saints* (Salt Lake City: The Deseret News Press, 1930)

Romney, Marion G., Oral History of Marion G. Romney, interviewed by James B. Allen in December 1972 and January 1973 as part of the Oral History program of the Church of Jesus Christ of Latter-day Saints.

Romney, Thomas C., *Life Story of Miles Park Romney*, Zions Printing and Publishing Company (1948).

Roy, Denny. "Kim Ho Jik: Korean Pioneer." *Ensign* 18 (July 1988): 18-23

Smith, Jesse N., *Journal of Jesse N. Smith: The Life Story of a Mormon Pioneer, 1834-1906* (Salt Lake City, Utah: Jesse N. Smith Family Association 1953)

Soares, Milton Jr., Interview of Milton Soares Jr. conducted by Helen B. Gibbons.

Taylor, Rebecca M., "Ah Mu: Generous Samoan Saint", *Ensign* (September 1999), pages 47 – 50

Teixeira, Ernani, "Narrative of Ernani Teixeira"

Udall, David King, *Autobiography of D. K. Udall*, (Arizona: Silhouettes 1959).

VanDenBerghe, Elizabeth S. "Edwin Dharmaraju: Taking the Gospel Home to India." Ensign 20 (April 1990): 60-62.

Watt, Ronald G. "Journal of Discourses" in Daniel H. Ludlow, ed., *Encyclopedia of Mormonism,* (New York: Macmillan, 1992)

Wells, John, Account of John Wells' conversion in *The Instructor*, (Salt Lake City: The Church of Jesus Christ of Latter-day Sints, 1944); pages 56–57

Zippro, John, Unpublished family history, LDS Church Family History library

Zippro, John, Interview with Francis M. Gibbons

Index

About the Authors

Francis M. Gibbons is the best-selling and most prolific Mormon biographer of the past century. He is a former full-time missionary, bishop, stake president, patriarch, secretary to the First Presidency, and member of the First Quorum of the Seventy.

Daniel Bay Gibbons is a former trial attorney and judge and is the author of one previous book. He has served as a full-time missionary, twice as a bishop, and as president of the Russia Novosibirsk Mission, the most remote mission on earth.

For author updates visit: http://www.danielbaygibbons.com/

32290267R00171

Made in the USA
San Bernardino, CA
13 April 2019